CONNECTICUT
MISCELLANY

ESPN, *THE AGE OF REPTILES*, COWPARADE & MORE

Wilson H. Faude

Charleston London

THE
History
PRESS

Published by The History Press
Charleston, SC 29403
www.historypress.net

Images are courtesy of the author unless otherwise noted.

First published 2013

Manufactured in the United States

ISBN 978.1.60949.890.0

Library of Congress CIP data applied for.

CONTENTS

CONTENTS

PREFACE

C onnecticut is a small state in size, but the riches and variety of the
sites and stories, the personalities and adventures it has to share are
unlimited. This book might be thought of as your "Connecticut Bucket
List." I hope you enjoy the journey and go and explore, to see firsthand all
that will unfold when you do.

Many, many individuals and institutions have made this book possible.
This book would not have made it to print without the loving, patient and
gentle counsel of my wife, Janet, who rescued her technologically challenged
husband more than once from the brink of the abyss. When available, our
son Paul and neighbor Tim Wheeler also helped.

The people at ESPN—Bill Rasmussen, Katina Arnold, Rich Arden, my
guide Arlyd Munoz-Snyder, the former senior vice-president Gary Perrelli,
Mike Solty and Jessica Gonzalez—were incredibly supportive and sharing.
Allen Phillips of the Wadsworth, Jennifer Sharp, Andy Hart and Pramode
Pradhan of the Hartford History Center gave invaluable assistance in
obtaining and scanning images. Rolf Anderson and Mrs. Anderson invited
me to the Leroy Anderson home and provided some of the images used in this
book. Todd Gipstein, president of the foundation that is preserving Ledge
Lighthouse, was generous in sharing information about the lighthouse. Bob
Gregson at Connecticut Tourism was always willing to answer questions and
search for images. Most of the information behind these chapters came from
personal visits to the places or with the subjects, and if other sources were
used, they have been credited in the text.

ESPN

How It Came to Be

This is a most improbable story. In fact, even if Hollywood stayed with the facts and accurately scripted it, one would nod in disbelief and say, "Nice idea but terribly overdone." But this *is* the story of ESPN.

In researching this chapter, I was provided with Bill Rasmussen's e-mail. He was the person who founded ESPN. I contacted him, and a date was arranged for me to call. My first question was simple: "Where did the idea for ESPN come from?" I was expecting something such as "around the kitchen table," "on a rainy afternoon," et cetera. He replied, "I was fired." I knew then that I had to start at the beginning.

William F. Rasmussen, Bill, was born on October 15, 1932, in Chicago, Illinois. As a youth, all he thought about was sports—first football ("I was too small") and then baseball ("It was baseball, baseball, baseball"). In June 1950, North Korea invaded the south, "and though I had an invitation to the Detroit Tigers farm club, there was no exemption for ballplayers, so I went to DePauw University and was in their air force ROTC." Following graduation in 1954, he was assigned to Eglin Air Force Base in Florida. In 1955, he married Lois Ann McDonald. At Thanksgiving at her parents' house, he was introduced to the vice-president of the Westinghouse Lamp Division. "I suspected that he had been invited by my in-laws hoping I would impress him and get a job."

Rasmussen did get a job and learned that at Westinghouse one could enroll at Rutgers in the MBA program and the company would pay half the tuition. If one graduated, it would pay everything. Perhaps the greatest thing he learned at Westinghouse was how much money was spent on advertising. He graduated from Rutgers in May 1959, had no college debt and, with $140 and two cohorts who contributed $140 each, started Ad Aid, Inc., in a vacant 800-square-foot building. Ad Aid, Inc., was a success. In July 1959 they added 2,500 square feet, and in October they moved to a 15,600-square-foot warehouse. In February 1960, they added another 14,300 square feet, but the work was seven days a week with long hours. Even though the client list included General Foods, S&H Green Stamps and Ballantine Beer, Rasmussen was bored and tired. On his thirtieth birthday he retired; his condition was that his partners pay him three years' severance. "I figured I could probably get a job in the first two, but if not I still had a year to find something to support my family."

His job search started when he bought a copy of *Broadcasting* magazine. There was an ad from a guy who was starting a radio station in Amherst, Massachusetts, advertising for a salesman and a sportscaster. Rasmussen drove to the station's headquarters in Westerly, Rhode Island. The owner met him. "Did you bring a demo tape?" he asked. "No," Rasmussen replied. "Have you done sportscasting before?" "No," Rasmussen answered. Something about Rasmussen impressed the owner to the effect that he told him, "If you can sort through all the FCC Rules and Regulations and get us on the air, you're my sports guy!" He did, and WTTT radio in Amherst went on the air. In 1965, Rasmussen moved to WWLP-TV in Springfield as sports director and later as news director. In 1974, he joined the New England Whalers as communications director. The Whalers did not make the playoffs in 1978.

On Saturday, May 27, 1978, at 11:00 a.m., Bill Rasmussen answered his phone. The voice on the line was Colleen Howes, wife of hockey legend Gordie Howe and referred to as the "Iron Lady of hockey." She managed her husband; she orchestrated the deal for their sons Mark, Marty and Gordie to play for the Whalers; and she, along with Howard Baldwin and Don Conrad, was the one in charge. In addition to his work with the Whalers, Rasmussen, since 1978, was the executive director of Howe Enterprises. "Bill, this is Colleen," he recalled her saying. "This is terrible. We're going to terminate your relationship with Howe Enterprises. Howard doesn't want you back either. I have to run and catch a plane."

"I had gone from worrying about my golf game to realizing I had been fired," Rasmussen said. "I was unemployed."

As Rasmussen thought about his next career, he wanted sports to be in it, and he wanted broadcasting serving the sports fan—or, as son Scott would label the fan, the "sports junkie"—twenty-four hours a day. "I sensed the thirst." Back in 1978, there was no CNN; in fact, one corporate chairman told Rasmussen, "In three years, there will be no cable television."

The plan developed with absolutely no map to guide it—for these were totally unchartered waters of every dimension in every direction. This network needed a name. It should have sports in it and entertainment. According to Bill, his son Scott "came up with ESP Network, for Entertainment and Sports Programming Network and a play on ESP." On June 14, 1978, Scott paid the fee, and ESP Network was incorporated. Their printer, Guy Wilson, made it ESPN and placed it in the elliptical oval.

The plan—the vision—began to evolve. RCA at the time had a transponder (communications satellite) and was hoping someone would reserve one of the twenty-four-hour channels to really get the "ball rolling." Rasmussen recalls, "Scott did the math and realized the great advantage of having a twenty-four-hour rate was less than the five-hour rate. Scott wanted to reserve three, but we eventually ordered one." RCA didn't need any money up front, so Rasmussen took a $9,000 advance on his credit card. Later, stuck in traffic on I-84 in an August heat wave, tempers simmering, Bill and Scott were batting around what to broadcast twenty-four hours a day. According to Bill, Scott blurted out: "Play football all day, for all I care."

Bill met with the firm K.S. Sweet, which after a time agreed to provide interim funding and to present a business plan to investors. There were seven on the list, and then Getty Oil was added as number eight. Bill kept making presentations. He flew to Los Angeles to Getty. That night, the hotel caught fire, and hours later he made the pitch on two hours sleep. There was a vice-president at Getty who wanted to be in television. Getty agreed to fund ESP Network. Bill was asked to prepare a ten-year cable projection and expected revenues and expenses:

> *At Getty, every prospectus was to outline the "first," "most likely" and "worst" projection for a project. Since there was nothing to base this on, I did my best. The review officer, after reviewing the projections, hurled them up in the air and yelled: "If this is the kind of projections…" in a tirade that lasted several minutes. We still, however, had the funding. But I was making it up as we went along, with what little facts and figures that were out there, which were few. Remember, there were no twenty-four-hour networks; ABC, NBC and CBS did not broadcast from one to seven o'clock in the morning. HBO was on only five hours a night, and CNN didn't exist.*

The site in Bristol was equally serendipitous. Jim Dovey of United Cable in Plainville contacted Rasmussen to tell him that Bristol had four parcels of

Satellite Dish Farm at ESPN, Bristol, Connecticut, February 6, 2013. *Joe Faraoni/ESPN Images*.

land (one and a quarter acres each) for sale. He only needed a sliver. Some were concerned if the site was appropriate for transmission. James Black of Scientific Atlanta, Inc., a major manufacturer of satellite dishes, et cetera, was brought in to review the site and present his findings. "Speaking before the Bristol Chamber of Commerce," Rasmussen recalled, "Black opened with 'Whoever picked this site (we held our breaths) couldn't have picked a better site, anywhere. It is an amazing site!'"

On September 7, 1979, at 7:00 p.m., Lee Leonard spoke into a live microphone before the television cameras: "If you love sports…if you *really* love sports, you'll think you've died and gone to sports heaven." ESP Network was on the air! It wasn't glamorous—two dishes, a small building, a trailer, a port-a-john—but it was on the air.

ESPN currently employs 6,500 individuals worldwide, 3,900 in Bristol. The Bristol campus is over 128 acres. It was the first to seriously employ female sportscasters, among them Gail Gardner, Linda Cohn, Robin Roberts and Chris McKendry. Sports Recap became Sports Center. Even before ESPN went on the air, Getty Oil exercised its 85 percent option, and shortly after the first broadcast, its representative began to cut the founders' salaries and duties. So they left. Scott was gone in October and Bill Rasmussen within the year.

Above: Studio F: Sports Center anchors Steve Levy and Linda Cohn on the set, November 15, 2012. *Joe Faraoni/ESPN Images.*

Right: Bill Rasmussen (left) with Bristol mayor Michael Werner at the groundbreaking ceremony for ESPN's Administration Center, 1980. *ESPN Images.*

Bill Rasmussen back on the set at ESPN, October 6, 2005. *Rich Arden/ESPN Images.*

The dream that Bill and Scott had is still very much in place, despite all the personnel machinations. The on-air journalists still research and write their own copy. In touring the campus, I was struck by the hundreds of individuals eagerly at work, focused and engaged. There are backup teams, scanning the globe for breaking news, doing research, keeping ESPN the premier sports network. The two satellite dishes now number more than forty, though one of the originals is still at the entrance. What started as one network is now seven nationally and some thirty-five globally, partially or wholly owned by ESPN. ESPN knows what its brand is, fiercely protects it (and proudly so) and never loses sight of its audience. From the very beginning, Bill Rasmussen's vision was simple: "To serve sports fans wherever sports are watched, listened to, discussed, debated, read about or played." It is ESPN's mission statement. He sensed sports fans' thirst, and he was right.

Today, ESPN is headed by George Bodenheimer. He started at ESPN some sixteen months after the founding, as a driver in the mailroom. Learning the company from the ground up, he is now the executive chairman. It may take a tough individual to run such a corporation, but it also takes a thoughtful one. Mr. Bodenheimer has openly reintroduced Bill Rasmussen to ESPN and its employees and acknowledges how Bill and Scott's vision and hard work changed the world of broadcasting with the words: "If you love sports…"

YOU HAVE A TWO-HEADED WHAT?

In 1792, the Connecticut legislature authorized the building of a new statehouse in Hartford. It was designed by Charles Bulfinch (1763–1844) and was his first public commission, followed by the Massachusetts Statehouse (completed in 1798) and the Maine Statehouse (completed in 1829). The two-story brick and brownstone Hartford State House was completed in 1796 in time for the legislative session on May 11. In addition to chambers for the Senate, the House of Representatives and the courts, there were offices for the governor, comptroller, treasurer, secretary of state and the school fund (board of education). On the third floor were committee rooms. In May 1796, Joseph Steward petitioned the legislature to use a third-floor room for a painting room. Permission was granted, and on June 6, 1796, Steward advertised in the *Connecticut Courant* that he "informs the public that he has opened a Painting Room in the State House."

Joseph Steward was born in Upton, Massachusetts. He graduated in 1780 from Dartmouth College and studied for the ministry under the Reverend Dr. Levi Hart (1828–1908) of Preston, Connecticut. By 1786, he was licensed to preach. Steward suffered from poor health and "bodily disorders." He was a deacon of the First Church of Hartford and compiled *The Hartford Selection of Hymns* in 1799. However, his ill health did not permit him to continue to serve as pastor of a church.

The painting room in the statehouse was not a success. The public may have agreed with William Dunlap's assessment of Steward's work: "Mr. Steward painted wretched portraits about and before this time in Hartford,

Connecticut. This gentleman had been (as I was informed at the time I saw him and his pictures) a clergyman. What turned him from the cure of men's souls to the characturing of their bodies, I never learned." Steward closed the painting room. On January 30, 1797, he advertised in the *Connecticut Courant* that he "takes the liberty to inform the public that he proposes, as soon as it can be accomplished, to make such a collection of natural curiosities and paintings as he hopes will gratify the curious." In May 1797, Steward successfully petitioned to use his former painting room "for depositing Painting, and Curiosities," and it opened in June 1797. Over the course of time, the museum had a number of names: Joseph Steward's Museum, the Hartford Museum and the Hartford Gallery of Fine Arts.

The popularity of Steward's Museum, with its curiosities, is evident from the listings in period newspapers. It should be noted that "curiosity" then signified an object of intellectual importance. In 1808, the museum outgrew the statehouse and moved a few blocks north to a seventy-foot-long gallery that Steward built onto his house. After Steward's death, the museum closed, and his widow and children received a portion of the collection. On January 6, 1824, the Hartford Museum reopened on Central Row across from the statehouse, "under an association of gentlemen," or subscribers, including the art patron Daniel Wadsworth (1771–1848). Newspaper advertisements continued to refer to the articles in the museum.

In 1840, the Hartford Museum closed, and shortly afterward, Daniel Wadsworth announced his intention to build the Wadsworth Atheneum two blocks south of the statehouse. It would have a "Gallery of Fine Arts" and would also serve as home to the Connecticut Historical Society, the Natural History Society and the Young Men's Institute (the Hartford Public Library). The Hartford Museum's collections were apparently scattered, although there is no known public record of their disbursement or sale. Many of the museum's paintings, including those by Steward, went to the Connecticut Historical Society, which publically exhibited them on April 21, 1840. The animals and scientific apparatus may have gone to the Wadsworth Atheneum, the historical society or one of the other tenants in the Wadsworth Atheneum.

The statehouse ceased to be the state capitol in 1878, when the government moved into its new capitol, designed by Richard Upjohn (1828–1903). The statehouse then became known as the Old State House, serving as city hall (1879–1915); as a community center for the Red Cross, war bond drives and local groups and as offices for the chamber of commerce and the Jaycees (1916–60); and as exhibition galleries for the Connecticut Historical Society

(1960–75). It was saved from demolition in 1975. From 1992 to 1996, the Old State House underwent a major multimillion-dollar stabilization and restoration that included new foundations, becoming ADA compliant, and the historic chambers were restored to their most documented periods: the Senate, 1796–1878; the House of Representatives as city council, 1878–1915; and the courtroom, 1920.

It was also decided to restore Joseph Steward's Museum to the building. The restoration of this, one of the earliest museums in the United States, was a challenge on many levels. Fortunately, the early research by Thompson R. Harlow of the Connecticut Historical Society had been carefully preserved. Historian William L. Warren found in the New Hampshire Historical Society Henry Ashley's diary of 1796–98, in which he recorded his visit to the museum in 1798:

> *In one Chamber is kept the Museum, kept by a Mr. Steward. I think I paid twenty cents for admittance. It contains four figures in wax work, a great number of portrait paintings, an Electrical Machine, with which we were Electrified, a number of Chinese Curiosities…several optical glasses as a Microscope, Prism, etc. There was the clothes that Col. Burnham wore in Algears, an Ostrich egg, the horn of an Antilope…and a number of Curiosities too numerous to mention here. The Museum is yet in its infancy but it was better than I expected.*

A gazetteer published in 1819 described the museum as "neatly arranged and handsomely filled with several thousand articles, such as paintings, waxwork, natural and artificial curiosities. Strangers and others, who visit the Hartford museum, will find a gratification for their curiosity and taste." Another useful source was a book of curiosities published in Boston in 1832 that identified hundreds of birds and animals and sites that were worthy of the term "curiosity." Various creatures were given their contemporary names; a cobra, for example, was listed as "the hooded snake from India." A most useful source was the notices that Steward placed in the local papers to attract an audience. Because a notice would often be repeated for six months to a year, one can have confidence that the items listed were indeed on view. According to the Harford *American Mercury* for May 3, 1804, the contents of the museum included: "A large elegant Historic painting. A likeness of Thomas Paine; and of Voltaire. A number of beautiful Birds and other Animals from the Island of Japan. A Calf with two complete heads; also a pig of the same description, having two perfect heads to one body; the sword from a sword fish."

Any restoration must embody a faithful reconstruction and evoke the spirit of the original; it must convey to today's visitors the same sense of wonder that a visitor would have had years ago. It must look as if it had always been there, warts and all. There must be items everywhere but with a sense of order.

Having assembled all possible information for the project, the task began of reassembling the items known to have been in Steward's Museum. The Connecticut Historical Society loaned many of the paintings by Steward to again hang in the museum. In the society's basement early electrifying machines were found. Steward advertised that he had "cloth made from the South Seas Island," and the Connecticut State Library had just such a piece of cloth received in 1840, the year the museum closed. There is no proof that this was from Steward's Museum, but the coincidence is compelling. Both the electrifying machine and the piece of cloth are now in the museum. The Children's Museum in West Hartford loaned a Bengal tiger, a mud puppy (a type of salamander), a period bird's egg cabinet and various shells and fossils. Nathaniel Reed, a prominent Florida businessman and a graduate of Trinity College in Hartford, contacted his friend Lieutenant Governor "Buddy" MacKay of Florida to secure an alligator. Thanks to the Florida Game and Fresh Water Fish Commission, one is again in the museum.

Steward noted that he had the "whole of *Wilson's Ornithology*." A copy of the book was found, and a list was made of all the birds mentioned. The United States Fish and Wildlife Service at the Rocky Mountain Arsenal in Commerce City, Colorado, agreed to loan many of the specimens in its possession. Thus, protected or endangered specimens, including a bald eagle, were secured legally. Many of the bird carcasses had been in the arsenal's freezer. They were shipped east, arriving in containers cooled by dry ice on Christmas Eve, when the contracted taxidermist was away. The cafeteria of a local insurance company agreed to store the cases in its walk-in freezer (contents unknown) until after the holidays. The specimens were later mounted and added to the museum.

For all of the success in finding items from public sources, the museum still needed hundreds of objects, especially rare and unusual animals, such as a two-headed calf. Following Steward's own practice, word went out that the public was invited to contribute items to the museum. The results were incredible. Rattlesnakes, a hooded snake from India, a mongoose and a cobra locked in mortal combat, a wild boar, bugs, beetles, butterflies, minerals, an ostrich egg, the horn of a unicorn, an eighteen-inch-long lobster claw, a porcupine, a three-horned goat, various skulls, a mummified hand, a camera

Steward's Museum as it looked in 2001, complete with his portraits, electrifying machines, a bald eagle, a three-horned goat and a bottle labeled "Tea thrown into Boston Harbor." *Courtesy Robert Benson Photography.*

obscura, a microscope, an 1820 barometer, a zagrascope, a silhouette machine, a wax head of Charles I of England and other curiosities were donated to the museum. One of the prized additions was a small papier-mâché terrestrial globe circa 1760, complete with its carrying case, which shows the constellations on the inside. A glass bottle has a paper label that reads: "TEA THROWN INTO BOSTON HARBOR, DEC. 16/1773" and contains something that might be tea. The bottle is similar to one in the collection of the American Antiquarian Society in Worcester, Massachusetts.

It was word of mouth that brought to the museum two of its greatest stars. Thanks to a friend of a friend, it was learned that a two-headed calf had been stillborn at the Golden River Dairy in Cheboygan, Michigan. The arrangements were made, and some six months later, the stuffed calf arrived. Knowing that a crate labeled "Contents: Two-Headed Calf" would probably not make it to the museum, the crate was simply labeled "household goods." Later, a visitor to the museum, Theresa Beck, learning of the need for a two-headed pig, tracked one down with skill and tenacity and donated it. Following Steward's example produced incredible results. In 1997, on the 200th anniversary of the museum's opening, 1,800 people lined up to see the two-headed calf. Major articles appeared in *People* magazine, *GQ*, national newspapers and various books and publications. Items would appear by mail or be left on the director's desk without warning. One day, two elderly ladies in a chauffeured car, on their way to Maine, stopped in, unannounced, to donate their grandfather's walrus tusks. Steward's Museum had caught the public's interest and imagination.

The documented "Calf with two complete heads" exhibit was restored to the museum in 1997. *Courtesy Robert Benson Photography.*

Today, visitors can climb the stairs of the Old State House and enter the doorway of Joseph Steward's Museum. The lighting is dim; from the ceiling hangs an alligator and various birds and animals. In cases and on tables there are scientific instruments, artifacts and fossils. Shelves are filled with electrifying machines, a bird's-egg cabinet and a blue heron in an eighteenth-century case. The portraits again hang near the ceiling, and there are all manner of curiosities—and yes, a two-headed calf and a two-headed pig.

WHERE IS THE ASYLUM OF HARTFORD'S ASYLUM STREET?

D r. Mason Fitch Cogswell was a nationally known Hartford surgeon and a founder of the Connecticut Medical Society. In 1804, he ligated the carotid artery "at a time when it had been attempted by no other surgeon in America." The Cogswells lived on Prospect Street in Hartford. In 1807, just before her second birthday, his daughter Alice contracted "spotted fever" (probably what is today known as cerebro-spinal meningitis) and became deaf. Her father immediately began a study of deaf education and found that there were no schools for the deaf in America. Near the Cogswells on Prospect Street lived a French Huguenot family, the Gallaudets. Their son, Thomas Hopkins Gallaudet, had graduated from Yale College and was a divinity student at Andover. In the spring of 1814, recovering from an illness, young Gallaudet was at his parents' home. Dr. Cogswell watched young Gallaudet interact with his daughter and saw that he had the patience and the caring to teach Alice how to communicate with other children. Cogswell gathered nine prominent citizens, and in one day they raised over $2,133 to begin the establishment of an American school for the deaf.

In June 1815, Gallaudet sailed to England to learn the art of teaching the deaf from the Braidwood family, who ran a school in London. The Braidwoods would share their methods of training teachers to teach the deaf only if compensated for every deaf child educated following their methods. In England, Gallaudet also met with the French Institute for the Deaf's noted director, the Abbe Sicard. According to Gary Wait, former archivist at the American School for the Deaf, he was developing a sign language based on the work of the Abbe de l'Epee, which may have originated from a monastic order in Spain whose members were pledged to silence. The Abbe's sign vocabulary and method from signs evolved from those used by the Paris deaf community and the French spoken and written language. The Abbe invited Gallaudet to come to Paris if the negotiations with the Braidwoods failed, which is what happened. Gallaudet went to Paris, where he studied to become a teacher for the deaf under the Abbe Sicard and his assistants, Laurent Clerc and Jean Massieu.

According to the late Winfield McChord Jr., executive director of the American School for the Deaf, there had not been enough time or funds for Gallaudet to stay in Paris and master all the techniques and skills needed to teach the deaf, so Gallaudet persuaded Clerc to come with him to America. In 1816, Gallaudet returned to Hartford with Clerc. On the voyage, Clerc taught Gallaudet sign language, and Gallaudet taught him English; together they began the development of an American sign language. The school was incorporated by the Connecticut General Assembly in May 1816, and the legislature appropriated $5,000 to the school. The formal name of the school was the Connecticut Asylum for the Education and Instruction of Deaf and Dumb Persons. On April 15, 1817, the school opened on the corner of Main and Mulberry Streets (now Main and Gold Streets) with 7 students, including Alice. By 1889, enrollment had grown to 162 students

On April 15, 1817, the school opened in rooms in this hotel at the corner of Main and Mulberry Streets. *American School for the Deaf.*

from Connecticut, Maine, Massachusetts, New Hampshire, Vermont and Rhode Island. In 1895, the school became known as the American School for the Deaf, or ASD.

In 1819, the U.S. Congress appropriated twenty-three thousand acres of public land in Alabama to be sold to benefit of the school. The land sold for $300,000, estimated to be some $6 million in today's value. The city of Birmingham now occupies the tract. With the funds, the school bought land in Hartford on what was known as Lord's Hill, just west of the present railroad station, and built a "modern" school building. The Litchfield Turnpike, the street in front of the new school, was renamed Asylum Street in the school's honor; Lord's Hill became Asylum Hill. The school remained there until 1921, when it sold the site to the Hartford Insurance Company and moved to West Hartford.

Gallaudet helped found the Institute for Living and other charitable institutions. Gallaudet College is named in his honor, and his son, Edward Miner Gallaudet, was its first president. In 1887, Daniel Chester French was commissioned by Gallaudet College to create a memorial to Gallaudet. The bronze sculpture portrays Gallaudet with young Alice Cogswell. Gallaudet is signing the letter "A." Alice responds with her right hand, making the letter

Daniel Chester French's statue of Gallaudet and young Alice Cogswell at the American School for the Deaf: "And with a look I hear." *American School for the Deaf.*

"A," while her left hand holds an open book: "And with a look I hear." The original is outside Chapel Hall at the college. In 1925, a second casting of the statue was made for the American School for the Deaf and sits prominently in front of the main building in West Hartford. French's plaster study for the statue is in the school's museum.

In 1922, French created the immortal statue of the seated Abraham Lincoln for the Lincoln Memorial. While a great deal has been written about the statue and Lincoln's hands, Mr. McChord expressed his thoughts about Lincoln's hands: "French remembered his earlier sculpture of Gallaudet and young Alice. He decided to position Lincoln's hands speaking in sign language to the deaf community with the letters 'AL,' for Abraham Lincoln."

The American School for the Deaf is still at 139 North Main Street in West Hartford. On May 2, 2012, it broke ground on a new sixty-thousand-square-foot education building. The school was a legendary pioneer on so many fronts: the birthplace of American sign language, the first school for the deaf in America, one of the first schools in the country to be racially integrated (1825) and the first school in the state to offer vocational training (1829). In 2017, it will celebrate its 200th birthday.

GOD IS THE BIGGER ELVIS

Christmas in Bethlehem, Connecticut

As I traveled along the Flanders Road in Bethlehem, I was struck at how rural the landscape was. My journey was to revisit the Abbey of Regina Laudis and to see its extraordinary eighteenth-century Neapolitan Crèche. The Abbey was founded in 1947 by Mother Benedict Duss, OSB, and Mother Mary Alice Trilles de Warren, OSB. Mother Benedict and Mother Mary had been nuns of the Benedictine Abbey of Notre Dame de Jouarre in France. Until the monastery of Regina Laudis was elevated in 1976 to an abbey, it was a dependent priory of Notre Dame de Jouarre, the seventh-century abbey northwest of Paris. The four-hundred-acre property that is the center of the Abbey was donated by Robert Leather. Though a "devout Congregationalist," he was concerned that the pine-covered hill would be subdivided and developed. He considered it a place of prayer and wanted it to be kept intact, forever, as a sacred place. The 1949 movie *Come to the Stable*, starring Loretta Young, was loosely based on the founding of the Abbey.

Today, the property is a complex of low-lying farmhouses, cottages, a blacksmith shop and a former brass factory that are behind high walls. There are orchards, beehives and livestock tended by the nuns. The Monastic Art Shop is open to the public (closed on Wednesdays) and offers crafts, food, pottery, woven and knitted goods and other items produced for sale. The Abbey's cheeses, honey, vinegar and herbs have been nationally acclaimed. Sister Noella Marcello, an artisanal cheese maker and PhD microbiologist in the study of cheese, was featured in the documentary *The Cheese Nun.*

The barn on the grounds of the abbey that contains the crèche.

On Flanders Road, a short distance from the Abbey, is a collection of three faded round gold signs. One is marked "Pax Crèche." The crèche was given to the Abbey by Loretta Hines Howard in memory of her husband in 1949. A short distance in, there is an eighteenth-century white barn, set quietly back amidst the trees, and a parking area. The barn belonged to Joseph Bellamy, an early Connecticut minister, and was given to the Abbey by Miss Caroline Woolsey Ferriday when she owned the Bellamy property. Outside is a simple sign: "Open 10–4."

One enters through the side door on the right. The interior is dimly lit. Ahead is the crèche. It is in a climate-controlled case, fifteen feet wide and ten feet high, set into the wide, far wall, wonderfully illuminated. In the center of the tableau is the Holy family. A rosy-cheeked Mary in pink silk presents the baby Jesus. They are not in a manger but beneath the ruins of a Corinthian column, a tribute to the most sacred place to Italians: Rome. Around them are the three kings with turbans, elegantly clothed, presenting their gifts. But the real drama is found in the surrounding figures of nobles, children, peasants, farm animals, camels, angels, merchants and peddlers, all who turn, pause and look at the Christ child. It is a majestic tableau, one with which anyone, of any

Villagers in the market pause to observe the presentation of the Christ child.

"station," could identify. The longer one stands and observes, the more the minute details and subtleties come into focus.

The figures have carefully sculpted terra cotta faces and hands and are between five to sixteen inches high. There are sixty-eight figures in the crèche. All are in their original eighteenth-century costumes. The crèche was crafted by artists in Naples, Italy, and presented to Victor Amadeus II, king of Sardinia, in 1720 as a coronation gift. After his death, it became the property of a family until it was brought to America in 1948. The Metropolitan Museum of Art's chief designer described the crèche as the "Rembrandt or Rubens" of crèches. The Metropolitan exhibits a similar crèche annually in the Medieval Sculpture Hall. It was given to the museum by the same Mrs. Howard, beginning in 1964. In 2005, the Abbey's crèche underwent a three-year restoration, directed by the Met's conservator, Won Ng. Despite the age, grime and insect infestation, the Abbey's crèche was, according to Ng, "pristine—never having been restored or exposed to old conservation techniques."

This was my second journey to the Abbey. The first happened many years ago at the invitation of Mother Jerome. I was the curator of the Mark

The Virgin Mary presents the Christ child before villagers, shepherds and the magi.

Twain House, and she invited me to view a photograph album of Twain at her family's villa in Florence, Italy. I arrived at the appointed hour and was shown into a small, plain, wood-paneled room that was divided by a slatted screen. Presently, Mother Jerome entered from the other side of the screen. She carefully placed the album on the turnstile and moved it to my side. Only then did she begin to converse. Most gently, she directed me to the pages that had the Twain photos. I was struck by this person of great presence, who was, I observed from her voice, of European ancestry and had apparently lived a very cultured life. Sometime after World War II, she entered the Abbey. It was only after her death in 2006 that I read her obituary and learned her story.

Born in 1908 as Melanie von Nagel, her father was part of the Bavarian court. As a serious and published writer, she was introduced to international society. She lived in Berlin, Cairo, Alexandria, Florence and New York. She married the artist Halil-berg Mussayassul. During the war, they gave shelter to refugees, including many concentration camp survivors. She spoke eight languages fluently. After the war, they came to live in New York. Her husband died in 1949. She stayed in New York writing and, most significantly, translating the works of the Romanian poet Paul Celan. She visited the Abbey and shortly thereafter, on March 18, 1957, entered as a postulant, noting, "I'm being led. Who else can plan the ways that rise from the roots to tip of meadow grass?" Her religious name came from Saint Jerome, who devoted his life to scholarship, teaching, writing and study. She was completely at peace with her world. As Mother Jerome, she was described as a "magnet for young and old, who sought out this woman of inspiration, hope, wisdom, humor and life." Mother Jerome died on June 27, 2006, at the Abbey.

Today, there is another nun at the Abbey who has attracted the notice of the press. Dolores Hart was a Hollywood actress who starred with Elvis Presley, Montgomery Cliff, Myrna Loy, Connie Francis, George Hamilton, Stephen Boyd and Anthony Quinn. She had visited the Abbey in 1959, when she wanted a break from a hectic performance schedule. She who received Elvis's first on-screen kiss, whose luminous blue eyes lit up the screen, walked away from it all in 1963 when she joined the Abbey. She had won a Theater World Award and a Tony nomination, but as she recalled, the earlier visit gave her "a sense of peace and inner renewal."

Today, she is the Mother Prioress at the Abbey, second in authority below the abbess, Mother David Serna. In 2010, she met with Archbishop Pietro Sambi, who asked her to consider making a film about monastic life. He thought people needed to understand it better. Her reported reply was: "Archbishop, it's been fifty years since I was in Hollywood. All my contacts are dead or gone." He answered, "Have no worries, Dolores. The Lord will find a way." She returned to the Abbey. Out of the blue, HBO called. The producer Sheila Nevins thought the Mother Prioress might make for an interesting documentary. *God Is the Bigger Elvis* shares life inside the Abbey, telling the stories of several nuns and even her own touching forty-seven-year friendship with her former fiancé, Don Robinson. The thirty-six-minute documentary is available from Amazon, et cetera. The film received an Oscar nomination for best documentary (short subject) in 2012. The Mother Prioress, who attended the ceremony in her nun's habit, commented, "It's absolutely an extraordinary event. Believe me, this is very different than being in a monastery." Unfortunately, the film didn't win.

Today, the Abbey is undergoing a major fundraising effort of more than $4 million for structural and code work that is badly needed. Included are upgrades to the fire and life safety systems, providing full accessibility for the handicapped and elderly and upgrades to housing units, among others. Anyone wishing to contribute can send a donation to the Mother Prioress, Abbey of Regina Laudis, 273 Flanders Road, Bethlehem, CT 06751.

When you drive Flanders Road, look for the circular gold disks citing the crèche or the Abbey itself. Walk around and visit the crèche, the store or the chapel. It is an appropriately peaceful and simple place. And that is the way it should be. It is not about us.

THE "WIDE-AWAKES"

Did They Elect Lincoln President?

In the early months of 1860, Connecticut Republicans knew their party was in trouble. The Democrats, under the leadership of Alfred E. Burr, publisher of the *Hartford Times* newspaper, were campaigning furiously to unseat the incumbent Republican governor, William Buckingham, and the Republican U.S. senator, James Dixon. Burr, as the publisher of the *Times* had transformed the paper from one with a meager circulation of four hundred to one of over two thousand. Nationally, Democratic presidential candidate Stephen A. Douglas, the senator from Illinois, was energizing his followers. Called the "Little Giant" (he stood only five feet, four inches tall), his campaign speeches were fiery and commanding, and he always played to full houses. The Republican Party had yet to find as dynamic a spokesman. It knew it faced certain defeat in the spring state elections and in the November presidential elections if it could not generate some excitement.

The party came up with two strategies. First, it extended invitations to nationally known Republicans to come to Hartford to speak. Second, it organized a group of young men to march with torchlights to escort the speakers and officials to drum up visible excitement. These two Hartford strategies changed the course of history.

O.R. Post, a Hartford Republican, learned that Lincoln would be speaking in New York City at Cooper Union on February 27, 1860. Post invited him to speak in Hartford. Lincoln had planned to travel to Exeter, New Hampshire, to visit his son Robert, who was a student at Phillips Exeter, and agreed to lecture in Hartford on March 5.

Lincoln's speech at the Cooper Union catapulted him onto the national stage. Finally, a Republican candidate was able to attract national press, and Republicans in Hartford understood the importance of building on that by making his visit here a great success. Two days before Lincoln was to arrive, Horatio Blair outlined a plan during a meeting in the rooms of J. Allen Francis at the corner of Main and Kinsley Streets. The idea was to organize a group of young men to escort Lincoln from place to place. To create the "buzz," Thomas Roberts, who had a stove and tinware shop on Kinsley Street, fashioned oil-fueled torches to swing in a fork at the end of a long pole. In the past, the torch at the end of a pole was in a fixed position. If the holder dipped it or carried it other than upright, the torch would go out. The Wide-Awakes' torches were different. The top part of the torch pole was split into a V. The lamp was then positioned in the V, on pins, so it would swivel and remain upright. This meant the torch would remain lit, regardless of the movement of the bearer or how it was carried. Since torches often leaked and stained the marchers' clothes, oilcloth was cut into capes to protect their clothes and cover their caps to shield their heads. The cape and cap created a uniform appearance that identified and distinguished the marchers. The shiny oilcloth fabric reflected the light from the torches, creating an even more festive image. When it came time to name this group, someone remembered a newspaper article describing the efforts to energize the party as "Republicans Wide Awake!" It was decided that this group would be known as the Wide-Awakes. Thirty-six young men signed up to escort Lincoln on his Hartford visit.

Lincoln's train arrived in Hartford at 7:20 p.m. It is important to remember the context of all this. It was March, after 7:00 p.m. and the sun had set. The light from the gas streetlights was marginal at best. As Mark Twain once observed, "Outside it was as dark and dreary as a house lit by Hartford gas."

Lincoln, who at six feet, four inches towered over most of the people there to greet him, stepped off the train at Hartford's Union Station. The Hartford Coronet Band in the lead, followed by the Wide-Awakes, torches blazing and the light reflecting off the shiny oilcloth capes and hats, created what one historian described as "an undulating river of Light, a magic-fire circle around the carriages carrying the speaker and the party tycoons." The Wide-Awakes escorted Lincoln's carriage to city hall on the corner of Kinsley and Market Streets, where he was to speak.

After 7:30 p.m., Governor Buckingham hushed the overflow crowd that had gathered on the third floor. An eyewitness described what it was like:

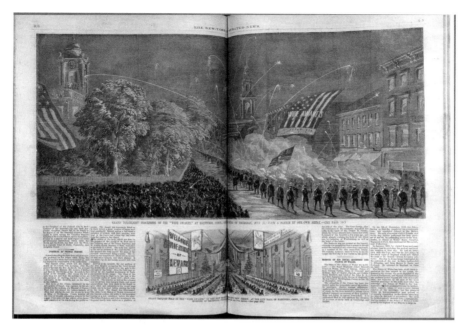

The *New York Illustrated News* published the "Grand Torch Light Procession of the Wide-Awakes at Hartford, Conn." on August 11, 1860. They are shown on Main Street. The Old State House on the left is being hit by a rocket. Center Church is on the right. It was an undulating river of light! *Richard Ring, Watkinson Library, Trinity College, Hartford.*

"When Lincoln rose to speak, I was greatly disappointed. He was tall, tall—oh, how tall! And so angular and awkward, that I had, for an instant, a feeling of pity for so ungainly a man." But as Lincoln spoke, he captivated the audience. "His face lighted up as with an inward fire…I forgot his clothes, his personal appearance and his individual peculiarities. Presently, forgetting myself, I was on my feet like the rest, yelling like a wild Indian cheering for this wonderful man."

As Lincoln ended the speech, "Let us have faith that right, eternal right, makes might, and as we understand our duty, so do it," the crowd cheered enthusiastically. The *Daily Courant* reported that the hall was crowded to excess and that the speech was "the most convincing and clearest speech we have ever heard…There was humor and fun interspersed so as to keep everyone good-natured and smiling."

After Lincoln finished, he was escorted to the home of Hartford's mayor, Timothy Allen, at 102 Asylum Street, today the site of Hartford 21, again preceded by the Hartford Coronet Band and the Wide-Awakes with their blazing torches. From that procession forward, no Republican parade anywhere was considered a success without the Wide-Awakes, and eventually, every Free State had a Wide-Awake chapter. The Hartford group finally added the word "original" to its title to mark its singular place in this phenomenon.

The next morning, Hartford's Republican leaders took Lincoln on a tour of the city, visiting the Sharps Rifle Manufacturing Co. on Capitol Avenue and the Colt Armory. In the early afternoon, Lincoln visited the Brown and Gross Bookstore, which stood at the corner of Main and Asylum Streets where a Burger King operates today. Inside, Lincoln met Glastonbury's Gideon Welles, editor of the *Evening Press*. A former Jacksonian Democrat turned Republican, Welles would become Lincoln's secretary of the navy.

On March 6, Lincoln boarded the 3:05 p.m. train for New Haven, where he would lecture before leaving the state, never to return. It has often been stated that the Original Wide-Awakes, the Hartford Wide-Awakes, elected Lincoln. What is true is that the Wide-Awakes created unparalled enthusiasm and excitement and, with their undulating river of light, brought real attention to Lincoln and the Republican Party. Governor Buckingham and Senator Dixon were reelected in the spring elections, and Lincoln was elected president in November.

COWPARADE STARTED HERE

Jerry Elbaum is a lawyer, an entrepreneur and a pioneer. After graduating from Cornell in 1957, he received his law degree in 1964 and was clerk to Judge J. Joseph Smith of the Second Court of the United States. In 1965, he went into private practice at Hartford's Yankee Brahmin firm of Robinson, Robinson & Cole. He was the first Jewish lawyer in the firm's history. Through a variety of circumstances and opportunities, he would be legal counsel to Perkins Machine and head of Smyth Manufacturing, and while working on a case for Chubb Insurance, he was crossing the hotel lobby where he saw two painted cows, nearly life size. They caught his attention and imagination. They were the invention of Walter Knapp, a window dresser in Zurich. Peter Hanig, the fashion shoe store owner in Chicago, had heard of the cows and decided they would be a great tourist draw for the former city of stockyards. They were introduced. Elbaum established the CowParade Holdings Corporation, and on June 15, 1999, Mayor Richard Daley opened the first American CowParade event. It featured 340 cows and was seen by an estimated ten million people. A bronze casting of a cow, in honor of the event, is in the city.

The cows were molded fiberglass and were created by Swiss-born sculpture Pascal Knapp; they are in three positions: grazing, standing and sitting. Some artists have, however, creatively altered the cows to perform daring feats, such as *Daisy's Dream*.

After the Chicago event, in 2000 there were CowParades in New York City; Samford, Connecticut; and West Orange, New Jersey. The New York

Above: Jerry Elbaum in CowParade headquarters. Beside him is a Las Vegas cow and behind him some of the CowParade figurines and collectables.

Left: *Daisy's Dream* was created by artist Randy Gilman for the New York CowParade. *Courtesy CowParade Holdings Corporation.*

event had 470 cows, 400 in the city and 70 in the boroughs. It was the first public art exhibition in the city to be in all five boroughs. FAO Schwartz held the opening event. An estimated forty-four million visitors saw the New York cows. One cow, *Twin Cowers*, celebrated the World Trade Center. The museum on the site will have the figurine of that cow, and it will be available in its museum store with all proceeds going to the museum. Since 1999, CowParades have been held around the world, everywhere from England and South Africa to New Zealand and Brazil (with an Olympic Cow) and from Tokyo and Las Vegas to Sydney—you name it. In 2003, CowParade came home to West Hartford, Elbaum's hometown.

After a CowParade is finished, the cows are auctioned to benefit a local charity. Thousands of cows and an excess of $30 million have been raised. In one case, for a Texas CowParade, a store commissioned a "longhorn" covered entirely in pennies. Titled *Penny Bull*, it is the work of Hartford artist Tao Labossiere. It was commissioned for the opening of a Vince Young Steakhouse Restaurant. Lucy Baines Johnson saw the sculpture and was determined that it would go to the auction. With a bit of negotiating, a second longhorn was created for the restaurant, and Ms. Johnson paid $150,000 at the charity auction. The sculpture is at the ranch and one day will go to the LBJ Presidential Library. Some of the artists who create the cows are from the area where the CowParade takes place. They submit a design, and if a sponsor likes it, the artist is then commissioned to "paint the cow." Artists or celebrities who have painted cows include Peter Max, Jan Saudic, Red Grooms, Richard Hass, Robert Stern, Ronnie Wood and Karim Rashid. People who "own" cows include Oprah Winfrey, Ringo Starr and David James. The more popular cows are often re-created into figurines of various sizes that are sold in stores and outlets worldwide. CowParade is a phenomenon that continues to grow and delight all viewers. It is the most successful, longest-running changing public art exhibition ever held.

THE USS *HARTFORD*

Ship and Submarine

There have been two United States naval vessels named in honor of Hartford, Connecticut. The first USS *Hartford* was a steam- and sail-powered sloop of war, commissioned in June 1859. It had a displacement of 2,790 tons and an overall length of 225 feet. It was designed to engage the world's most modern and capable warships of the day.

After its christening, it sailed the waters of Hong Kong and China as the American flagship of the East India squadron. With the outbreak of the Civil War, it was ordered home and became the flagship of the Western Gulf of Mexico Blocking Squadron under Admiral David Farragut. It was in many naval actions, including the Battle of Vicksburg and the capture of New Orleans. During the campaign to block the South from using the Gulf of Mexico, Farragut sailed into Mobile Bay. The Confederates had filled the waters with mines (torpedoes). His famous order "Damn the torpedoes, full speed ahead!" turned the tide of battle and resulted in a decisive Union victory that contributed to deterring foreign powers from aiding the Confederate states. It also captured the public's imagination.

After the war, the USS *Hartford* served in the Asiatic Fleet and in South America. It was later used as a sail-training vessel until its decommissioning in 1926. After its decommissioning, many of its parts were scattered as trophies. The prow of the ship was removed and placed in a case in the Connecticut state capitol. Its anchor, a bell and other items were "permanently loaned" by the U.S. Navy to the city of Hartford. In 1950, at the request of Trinity College's president, G. Keith Funston, the City of Hartford placed on the campus, as

"An August morning with Farragut; the Battle of Mobile Bay, August 5, 1864." William Heysharm Overand, artist. *Wadsworth Atheneum.*

a memorial to the more than one hundred Trinity men who had served in the Civil War (eighty-one Union, twenty-four Confederate), two of the USS *Hartford*'s cannons. The cannons today flank the statue of the Right Reverend Thomas Church Brownell, the college's first president. When the second USS *Hartford* was commissioned in 1994, the navy league refurbished them and had them mounted on authentically designed carriages for the ceremony, after which they returned to the college. Its anchor is on the campus of the University of Hartford, seasonally painted by graduating students.

The second USS *Hartford*, SSN 768 submarine, was in 1994 Electric Boat's fifty-seventh ship of the improved Los Angeles Class nuclear-powered attack submarine. It was equipped with the highly accurate AN/BSY-1 sonar and weapons control system, sophisticated torpedoes and Harpoon anti-ship missiles and could launch Tomahawk cruise missiles. It is 362 feet in length, and its displacement (surfaced) is 6,127 tons and (submerged) 6,900 tons. On December 4, 1993, Laura O'Keefe christened the ship: "In the Name of the United States, I christen thee *Hartford*. May God bless her and all who sail in her."

In April 1993, Commander George D. Kasten reported as commanding officer of USS *Hartford* (SSN 768). Born in Illinois, he graduated in 1975

Christening ceremony for the USS *Hartford* (SSN 768), December 1993. At the top of the submarine's sail are (from left to right) Commander Kasten and Lieutenant Commander Hanley; just below them is Paul DaQui, chair of the commissioning committee. *U.S. Navy.*

from the University of Utah through the Navy Enlisted Scientific Education Program with a BS in mechanical engineering. After completing nuclear power training and basic submarine training in October 1976, he reported to the USS *Narwal* (SSN 671). Various other commands followed until his assignment as to the USS *Hartford* (SSN 768).

One of the things that distinguished Commander Kasten was that he took seriously the importance of establishing a connection and a relationship between the USS *Hartford* (SSN 768), its officers and crew and the city for which it was named, its citizens and its institutions. He personally introduced himself to city leaders and involved his crew in the schools and other activities. Local businessman Paul J. DaQui took on the role of chairing the commissioning committee and further broadened the outreach. On November 1, 1994, the construction and fitting out of the submarine was completed, and it was delivered to the navy. On November 15, I was invited

The author with Commander Kasten in the sail, returning to New London, November 15, 1994.

by Commander Kasten, with others, to join him and the crew on a short trip into local waters. It is very, very hard to comprehend the actual size of such a ship and how essential it is to have a disciplined and coordinated crew, twenty-four hours a day, until one has been aboard, submerged, et cetera. It is awesome to stand in various spaces and watch the officers and crew go about their duties. It was a privilege to stand in the sail, the tower that rises from the submarine, as one returned to New London Harbor and the Groton submarine base. One can be justly proud of these servicemen.

On December 10, 1994, the USS *Hartford* (SSN 768) was commissioned. The commissioning ceremony marks the formal acceptance of a ship as a unit of the operating forces of the United States Navy. At the beginning of the ceremony, the ship flies no colors; platform guests are announced, but no naval honors are rendered. To place the ship in commission, the commissioning officer reads the commissioning directive, the national anthem is played and flags are raised. These flags are the national ensign on the aft staff, the jack on the forward staff and the commissioning pennant on the aft end of the sail. (Navy lore relates that the commissioning pennant dates back to the seventeenth century, when a Dutch admiral hoisted a broom at his masthead to symbolize to the enemy English his intent to sweep them from the sea. The English admiral responded by hoisting a horsewhip to chastise the Dutch.) The commissioning pennant is therefore a long, narrow strip symbolizing the horsewhip. It is blue at the hoist with a union of seven white stars and a horizontal red and white stripe at the fly. It remains with the ship until it is decommissioned. The commanding officer then reads his orders and assumes command of and responsibility for the ship. Since its commissioning, it has been deployed around the globe. According to the navy, it is supporting "national security and maritime security interests."

THE DUTCH TREATY OF 1650 AND ADRIAEN'S LANDING

A major development in Hartford is named Adriaen's Landing. It contains a convention center, a Marriott Hotel and the Connecticut Science Center. It is appropriate to know who Adriaen was and why the name "Adriaen's Landing" was given to the area. The short answer is that Adriaen Block was a Dutch explorer, and there was a Dutch settlement in Hartford. The English settlement of Connecticut might not have happened in Hartford if the Dutch had not been here first. Even so, that is not the reason the area was named Adriaen's Landing.

The Dutch exploration of the New World began in 1609, when the Dutch-owned United East India Company employed the Englishman Henry Hudson to search the Americas for the Northwest Passage to Asia. It was believed that such a passage must exist, and when found it would provide a shorter and less costly trade route to the riches of Cathay. His explorations established the Dutch claims in the region.

While he did not find the elusive Northwest Passage, he did discover an abundance of "many skins and peltries, martins, foxes, and many other commodities," according to historians Ross Hatch and Russell Shorto. After Hudson's death in 1611, Dutch merchants sent Hendrick Christianson and Adriaen Block to formally establish the fur trade.

They did, and the Dutch West India Company was given a monopoly over trade in Africa and America. In 1626, the company bought Manhattan Island for twenty-four dollars, in what may be history's most famous real estate deal, and established a settlement called New Amsterdam. The symbol of the settlement was the beaver. To understand how lucrative the fur trade was, one record lists over eighty thousand beaver pelts and over nine thousand otter pelts shipped from New Amsterdam to Holland in a ten-year period.

Block charted Long Island Sound and part of the Connecticut River. In 1633, the Dutch built a small fort in Hartford, where three rivers meet (the Connecticut, the Hockanam and the Freshet River, today known as the Park River). The purpose of the fort was to serve as an outpost to receive the thousands of furs that the Indians and others brought to trade with them. The fort was a modest structure, thinly manned on approximately thirty acres of land. Twice a year, when the river was full, Dutch ships would sail up from New Amsterdam to pick up the furs.

The arrival of the English from Cambridge to Hartford in 1636 changed everything. While some may have come for religious reasons, it is no coincidence that the presence of the Dutch fort determined that this was the place to establish a permanent inland English settlement. Once established, early accounts record growing issues between the men in the fort and the English settlers. Stray Dutch cattle eating English crops further elevated tensions. As more and more Englishmen settled, Dutch lands were encroached upon.

It became apparent to the leaders of the English and the Dutch that something had to be worked out to avoid a war. After much negotiating, it was agreed that the governors of the Plymouth Colony, the Massachusetts Colony, the Connecticut Colony and the New Haven Colony should meet with the Dutch representatives. The governors wanted to hold the meeting in Boston, but the Dutch preferred Manhattan, so Hartford was selected because it was between the two. The Dutch were represented by none other than Peter Stuyvesant, "Governor General of the New Netherlands, Curacao, Aruba and etc.," who was accompanied by his English secretary, George Baxter, and a large entourage.

Stuyvesant set out from Manhattan on September 17, visited Dutch settlements along the way and arrived in Hartford on September 21, 1650. The English greeted him cordially and wined and dined him. The resulting Hartford Treaty of 1650 formally solidified the English position. While the Dutch could retain their fort in Hartford, the remaining lands on both sides of the Connecticut River were declared English. A boundary line was drawn between the English and Dutch interests to prevent an invasion by the English on Dutch territory. It ran north–south through Long Island and the mainland, at the west side of Greenwich Bay. (This is why there are English-

and Dutch-named counties on Long Island, Suffolk and Nassau.) No Dutch house could be built within ten miles of the line. Any disputes would be mediated by the Dutch in Manhattan and the colony of New Haven.

Stuyvesant knew he did not have the military strength to defeat an English invasion from the north, so a treaty that recognized Dutch interests around Manhattan was all he could hope for. The treaty was formally signed, and on October 12, 1650, Stuyvesant left Hartford.

Two years later, England and Holland went to war. After news reached Hartford on June 27, 1653, Captain John Underhill, with a small group of men, stormed the fort, threw out the Dutch and proclaimed, "I, John Underhill, do seize upon this house and land hitherto belonging as Dutch goods, claimed by the West Indian Company of Amsterdam…for the state of England." The colonial court ordered Underhill not to sell the fort and its land, but on July 18, 1655, he did just that. He sold the fort and its thirty acres to Richard Lord and William Gibbons. The Dutch were powerless to retake the fort. Upset at the ouster, the Dutch referred to the settlers in Hartford as "Jankes," pronounced Yankees, which meant thief, robber or pirate.

It was the Dutch fort erected at the cross rivers of the fur trade in Hartford that dictated a new English settlement should be built there. When Hartford was chosen as the site for colonial leaders to meet and resolve their issues, the city assumed the mantle of a respected place.

Notwithstanding the above history, that is not why the area was called Adriaen's Landing. In 1995, Robert Fiondella, head of the Phoenix Companies, hired architect Bill Mead to draw up plans for a major development on the land owned by the company between Columbus Boulevard and the Connecticut River. Comprising some thirty acres, it envisioned amenities (a hotel, a stadium, a science or aquarium center, et cetera) that would be a stimulus to the economy and create jobs and an enhanced profile for the city and the region. After being given an early presentation by Bill Mead of the plans, I asked him why the name Adriaen's Landing for the site. He replied, "As you know, my wife, Hansi, is Dutch, so I named it after her ancestry."

THE CONNECTICUT FIRST AND SECOND COMPANY, GOVERNOR'S FOOT GUARD

Proud Traditions

They are quintessential Connecticut. In their resplendent scarlet coats with silver and black facings and towering bearskin caps, they have escorted, protected and represented the best of our state for more than two hundred years. They are the oldest organized military organization in the country. And if it hadn't been for a drunken indiscretion by others, they might never have been formed at all.

In colonial times, it was customary for a group of Hartford men to be enlisted and trained as a military unit whose sole purpose was to escort the newly elected governor and members of the General Assembly on election day. The day was traditionally marked with great festivities, the imbibing of spirits notwithstanding. On election day in 1768, the escort company apparently imbibed a little too much and staggered and jostled the dignitaries it was supposed to be protecting. The reaction to the "disrespect and indignity" shown to the elected officials put an end to the troop. For the next two elections, the honor of escorting the officials was given to Captain George Pitkin's company from East Hartford. (It was common for well-to-do individuals to have their own private corps of trained soldiers under their command.) Hartford's pride was sorely wounded, and a group of civic-minded young men vowed to return the escort honor to Hartford.

In October 1771, they petitioned the General Assembly to form the Governor's Guard to guard the governor and the General Assembly. The petition was granted on October 19.

The First Company elected as its first commandant Samuel Wyllys. Age thirty-two and a graduate of Yale, his father and grandfather had been secretary of the colony of Connecticut. As a colonel in three state regiments, he saw action in battles in Boston, Long Island, White Plains and the Hudson highlands before retiring in 1781 to become the brigadier general of the Connecticut militia. In 1771, he married Ruth Belden Stoughton, whose name would be adopted for the Ruth Wyllys chapter of the Hartford Daughters of the American Revolution. According to John Caldwell, Samuel Wyllys was responsible for choosing the distinctive uniform of the Governor's Foot Guard: their scarlet coats, silver and black facings and bearskin caps. In 1665, when the colony of Connecticut and the colony of New Haven became one colony, the new united colony had two capitals, one in Hartford and one in New Haven. The legislature would meet in the fall in New Haven and in the spring in Hartford. In time, New Haven decided it should have its own Governor's Foot Guard, and a group of sixty-five young men met in New Haven at Beer's Tavern on December 27, 1774. Thereafter, the Hartford troop became known as the First Company, Governor's Foot Guard, and the New Haven troop as the Second Company, Governor's Foot Guard.

The Second Company, Governor's Foot Guard, owes its formation to Benedict Arnold, whose leadership also resulted in his election as its first captain. Other notable members included Aaron Burr, vice president under Jefferson; Ethan Allen, who led the forces that captured Fort Ticonderoga; and James Hillhouse, who served for sixteen years as a federal senator from Connecticut. When the news of the Battle of Lexington reached New Haven on April 21, 1775, fifty-eight members of the Foot Guard voted to go to Cambridge to assist their fellow Patriots. On April 22, Arnold assembled the guard on the New Haven green and demanded from the selectman the key "to the King's Powder." The selectman was reluctant, but legend shares that Arnold forcefully declared, "None but the Almighty God shall prevent my marching." The selectman relented, and Arnold received the key, allowing him and the guard to take powder, ball and flint with them to fight in Boston. Since 1904, the guard has celebrated "Powder House Day" in New Haven.

Since its inception, the Foot Guard has escorted the greats and near greats at important Connecticut and national events. It escorted General Washington and Governor Trumbull in September 1780 when the American forces first linked with the French armies in America. Meeting on the green in front of Hartford's meetinghouse, today the site of the Old State House, the Foot Guard provided a vivid splash of color against the white uniforms of the French troops under the Comte de Rochambeau and the dark blue of the regular American troops. Every September, the Foot Guard reenacts this event, often with French dignitaries participating. When President John Adams passed through Hartford on August 2, 1798, the Foot Guard assembled and performed its duties with less than two hours to get ready. Adams was the first of many presidents the guard would escort. When the Marquis de Lafayette visited in 1824, he noted that the Foot Guard was "equal in discipline and appearance to any company I have ever seen."

The Foot Guard has been invited to march in numerous presidential inauguration parades. Perhaps the most difficult was that of John F. Kennedy in 1961. It had snowed, was bitter cold and a railroad strike had forced everyone to make alternate plans. True to form, the Foot Guard found transportation to Washington and secured accommodations through the Washington Gas Company. The newly fallen snow made the Foot Guard's uniforms even more distinctive as they marched escorting Lieutenant Governor John Dempsey.

In 1892, Connecticut's governor, Morgan Bulkeley, rode his white horse escorted by the Foot Guard in Chicago. Bulkeley hoped that a strong impression might foster his interest in securing the Republican nomination for president. The guard and the governor were a huge success with the crowds. When it was announced that for the next day's parade, whether out of jealousy or politics, all politicians would be escorted by national troops in their drab brown uniforms, Bulkeley declared that if the Foot Guard could not escort him, he would swear them all in as members of his staff and prevail. The committee relented, and the Foot Guard escorted Bulkeley—but the Republican nomination went to Benjamin Harrison.

In modern times, the Foot Guard remains a symbol of our state. When President Kennedy received an honorary degree from Yale in 1962, the Foot Guard escorted him. When Queen Elizabeth II visited Connecticut in 1976, the Foot Guard escorted her. When Madame Jihan Sadat of Egypt received an honorary degree from the University of Hartford in 1983, the Foot Guard escorted all of the dignitaries, scarlet uniforms dazzling in the darkness of the Lincoln Theater. When the Old State House celebrated its 200th birthday in 1996, the Foot Guard led the all-state parade. It organizes and holds the governor's Inaugural Ball. On the Saturday and Sunday before St. Patrick's Day, in Hartford and New Haven, respectively, the companies lead the parades. They represent the best of our state, in good times and in bad, with pride, discipline and that indelible dash of color. No other state has a Foot Guard of equal stature or longevity. You hear their bands at great events; you watch as the troops, led by the commandants and color guards, sweep the crowd with unmistakable pride and joy. You can be a part of it, stand beside presidents and dignitaries and enjoy the comradeship of the men and women who help ensure that this tradition is alive and well. If interested, go to their websites and learn how to sign up and become a vital member of the uniquely Connecticut tradition.

WALLACE NUTTING

Reinventing America

Wallace Nutting (1861–1941) would have been a totally forgettable person had he remained a Congregational minister serving modest congregations. The world in the 1890s saw the creation of a new America. New inventions and products were produced to please and pleasure the consumer. Nutting became an enthralled consumer of the leisure commodities. When bicycling became popular, he pedaled; when the camera was all the rage, he bought one and carried it with him. The limitations of the pulpit constrained him, so in 1904, at the age of forty-three, he retired. His new occupation was to enjoy the goods and pleasures of the consumer culture that was overtaking America. In 1913, captivated by the American automobile, he purchased a Stevens-Duryea Tourer. When he could afford to, he hired a chauffeur. Not content to be just a consumer, he dedicated his energies to shaping the consumer to buy his products on a hitherto unparalleled scale.

President Calvin Coolidge said it best: "The chief business of the American people is business." Wallace Nutting, with his ministering background, made it his new profession to preach to all the romantic ideals of small-town New England and his views of "Old America" and to sell his products. He began collecting early American furniture from the seventeenth and eighteenth centuries and then made copies of the furniture and marketed them as representative of Old American values. He branched out into prints, travel books, house restorations and cultural tourism. While preaching to save the cultural soul of America, at the same time he capitalized on the new American "resources" and those who could afford to buy his products.

To his credit, Nutting toured New England and sought out early furniture for his collection. He established workshops where the furniture would be faithfully reproduced to allow contemporaries to have pieces of Old America. In his commercial texts, he proffered complete disdain for the machine and modern technology. In reality, he used the machine to reproduce furniture, and his craftsmen were skilled cabinetmakers using modern construction techniques. He built his entire business on modern technology and mass consumption while posturing that his historic reproductions were solutions to contemporary social ailments. He created historical themes and romantic

Wallace Nutting, by William Cushing Loring, believed to have been commissioned by Nutting to accompany his collection when it went to the Wadsworth Atheneum. *Wadsworth Atheneum.*

vignettes on the values of Old America and rural New England with the clear statement that owning a Nutting piece would be good for one's soul, reflect on one's values and enhance one's life. The Wallace Nutting line of goods was the right stuff for later-day pilgrims and their homes.

Perhaps the best known of all of Nutting's products were the hand-colored prints. The subjects ranged from landscapes to quaint vignettes of a gentle lady sitting in an old-time setting doing something purposeful, such as mending. Nutting carefully composed the pictures, took the photographs and then hired colorists to carefully hand color the platinum prints. To be sure each print was colored exactly the same way, he wrote out precise instructions: "Sky: Prussian Blue and Chinese White," et cetera. Though the prints were mass-produced, he took great pains to point out that each was "hand colored."

Nutting was the mass marketer. He was the pastor who understood what his flock needed, and he understood how to appeal to their senses. His advertisements were unabashed statements that "Nutting knows best," and his appetite to control all aspects of his Old American vision was as voracious as

"An Afternoon Tea," circa 1916, hand-tinted platinum print, Wallace Nutting. *Wadsworth Atheneum.*

his marketing zeal. Behind the bespeckled silver hair was a controlling tyrant. In an era when Americans did want to be told what to do, Nutting furnished the direction: "Pictures on the Walls Make a House a Home—Wallace Nutting Hand-colored Pictures"; "Wallace Nutting Furniture—Beauty, Construction, Style"; "Wallace Nutting Window Displays Work Wonders"; "The birthplace of Distinctive American Art—Wallace Nutting Hand-colored Pictures." He developed the first states' beautiful books, *Maine Beautiful* and *New York Beautiful*. They were designed for the motoring consumer who would then have to have a Nutting piece of furniture, print or another book. With his furniture, he promoted his prints; in his prints, he featured his furniture; in his books, he featured his collection and those of the known superstars: the Metropolitan Museum, the Wadsworth Atheneum, the National Gallery of Art and prestigious collectors. The cross marketing of his goods and products was relentless.

Nutting's early collecting and scholarship on American furniture established a standard and respect for early American furniture that remains today. His *Furniture Treasury*, first published in 1928 in two volumes, contained over five thousand illustrations. Yet despite his collecting and scholarship, his all-pervasive marketing made many dismiss Nutting as merely a marketer and promoter and not a serious collector or scholar. Detractors considered him one who bought minor pieces but marketed them in a major way. His collection at the Wadsworth presents one of the most complete collections ever assembled on early American furniture and decorative accessories, and it was assembled before many regarded the subject worthy of discussion. Nutting changed the public perception of early American furniture. As part of his evangelical approach to the values of Old America, he told the American public why the early furniture was good and worthy of their respect.

When Nutting no longer needed his collection of original furniture, he arranged to sell it to J.P. Morgan Jr. for eventual placement at the Wadsworth Atheneum. Here again was Nutting at his best. First, he arranged to sell his collection to a Morgan, thus creating instant respect for him and his collection. Then he arranged for the collection to be given to the prestigious Wadsworth Atheneum. Then, in books and publications, advertisements and promotions, he referenced the Wallace Nutting Collection at the Wadsworth Atheneum, given by J.P. Morgan Jr. The cross-marketing promotions that we take for granted today were first created on the large scale by Nutting.

The first exhibition of the collection was installed by Nutting himself in the basement of the Morgan Building of the Wadsworth in 1928. There he created period room interiors, showcasing his collection. When its Avery Building was completed in 1934, part of the collection was reinstalled on the second floor by director "Chick" Austin and architectural historian Henry Russell Hitchcock. They neatly lined the furniture and accessories along the walls, treating the pieces as modern masterworks to be seen singly. In 1967, curator Henry Maynard organized the exhibition "Connecticut Furniture, Seventeenth and Eighteenth Centuries," which featured the Nutting Collection and brought new scholarship and respect to the era. Later, curator William Hosley reinstalled the Nutting Collection in the permanent galleries. He also curated the mammoth exhibition: "The Great River, Art & Society of the Connecticut Valley, 1635–1820" in 1985, in celebration of the state's 350th anniversary. This put the collection in the larger context of the Connecticut River Valley. In 2003, curator Thomas Denenberg curated the special exhibition "Wallace Nutting and the Invention of Old America," which was accompanied by his definitive book, of the same title, on Nutting and the collection.

Nutting was of his era. Nutting sold the values of rural New England and "Old America" as his way to make money—lots and lots of money. When the public did not know the importance of early American furniture, he educated them. He understood America, the public and his own desire to have the resources to enjoy life with all of its benefits and amenities. Denenberg put Nutting in that context. And while Nutting preached, "Whatever is new is bad," he did so comfortably from his glistening chauffeur-driven Stevens-Duryea Tourer. It is indeed what Nutting was all about.

EVERETT RAYMOND KINSTLER

Painter of Presidents, Hollywood and Trashy Novels

E verett Raymond Kinstler, known to his friends as Ray, was born in New York in 1926. As a teenager, he was drawing covers for magazines and lurid novels, the ones with busty maidens falling out of their unbuttoned gowns or buccaneers who were fully equipped. His pulp illustrations are in the hundreds, and at one time, a three-panel screen in his New York studio was upholstered with the most evocative examples of his work. That was the very screen behind which first ladies, dignitaries and other sitters would change into the outfits for their portraits. When asked what a sitter's reaction was when he or she emerged, Ray only shared a wry smile. Those commissions helped support him early in his career and later let him enjoy a less conservative, more playful but no less professional aspect of his craft. He studied at the Art Student League and in 1974 was elected to the National Academy of Design. As a portrait painter, he has painted the greats and near greats. He has painted more cabinet secretaries than any other artist. He has painted seven presidents—Nixon, Ford, Carter, Reagan, George H.W. Bush, Clinton and George W. Bush—and his portraits of Presidents Ford and Reagan are the official White House portraits. He has written numerous books on his portraits, the art of portrait painting, various examples of his work and more. A general count of the number of portraits is over 1,200. The National Portrait Gallery has 75 of his portraits, and he is in the collection of the Metropolitan Museum of Art, the Brooklyn Museum and others. In 1999, he was awarded the Copley Medal from the Smithsonian, its highest honor.

Kinstler painting the official White House portrait of President Gerald Ford in Vail, Colorado. Kinstler recalled, "I've painted President Ford twelve times…and he said he wanted me to keep trying." *Courtesy Everett Raymond Kinstler, used with permission.*

We sat in his lofty studio in western Connecticut that he built over the tennis court. The studio was carefully sited. One wall was due north and appropriately almost entirely of glass. On the easel was a work in progress surrounded by tubes and pots of paint, cloths, brushes, cleaners and various tools of the trade. A sitter's platform was ahead on the right. The walls had copies of various portraits: Tom Wolfe in his white suit; Christopher Plummer as Prospero; and Katharine Hepburn, to whom he refers as the "West Hartford girl," in reference to where I, among others, live. A comfortable sofa and a few chairs were off to the side, beneath a balcony, creating a place to talk and relax. A coffee table was stacked with various books and articles. Two elderly retrievers were comfortably sprawled on the floor, awaiting another milk bone.

The conversation is engaged, rapid, open. It is always a pleasure to be with someone who is very good at what he/she does, who is confident

Ray Kinstler in his Connecticut studio. It is a comfortable and creative space. The walls share various copies of his portraits.

and friendly but not arrogant. With a crackling sense of humor, it is clear that painting portraits has kept him eighty-seven years young. For a sampling of his work, search Everett Raymond Kinstler. There one will find a whole gallery: John Wayne in western gear; Katharine Hepburn in various poses, including in slacks with a canvas cap, shown on the mantel of her town house with her four Oscars; Paul Newman; Salvador Dali; Tennessee Williams; Gregory Peck; Betty Ford; Marion Anderson; Leonard Bernstein; presidents; cardinals; and many regular folks, as well as astronauts, government officials, bankers, judges and friends. And one will find Cowboy Andy, the art for *Romantic Love* and other pulp gems. As Tony Bennet said, "I don't think there is a better portrait painter since Sargent. Kinstler is that good." He captures the visage and, more importantly, the character, essence and spirit of the sitter.

We talked about the evolution of a commission. He shared some of the process, how he needs to know if this is an official portrait of a bank officer or a college president or for the White House, government office or a home. Where is it expected to hang, and what are the elements of that site: lighting,

Marion Anderson's portrait, by Everett Raymond Kinstler. Music critic Blyth described her voice as "a rich vibrant contralto of intrinsic beauty." *Courtesy Everett Raymond Kinstler, used with permission.*

the walls, height. What, if any, are the symbols or objects (a college mace, doctoral robes, a baseball bat, a walking stick, et cetera) that may be desired to be included. He seeks to resolve as many of these questions so he can get on to doing what he lives for—to paint. He meets with the subject, and he or she talks as he sketches. The composition evolves. He reflects inwardly on the work, the background, the "props," the placement and that all-important factor, the lighting.

Ray has been generous of his time and talent, helping to raise support for various New York institutions, including the Players Club and the National Arts Club, by creating special edition lithographs of appropriate celebrities or gold medal winners. For Players, he did one of James Cagney that was so well received it was decided to do another to help support the club's library. Katharine Hepburn seemed an ideal choice, and various efforts were made to contact her and see if she would agree to the idea. One hot summer day in New York, Ray was in his shorts, dripping, when the phone rang. "Mr. Kinstler?" the halting Yankee voice asked. "This is Miss Hepburn. If you can get up here in the next thirty minutes, I'll consider your idea." In a flash, he dressed, dashed out the door, grabbed a cab and went to her town house. He explained the project and that all sales would support the library. He heard footsteps, and her niece came into the room. He was asked to repeat the description of the project. When he'd finished, her niece snapped, "Isn't Players the club that has only men as members?" "I assumed that every egg in the place had cracked and that the project was doomed." Miss Hepburn spoke: "Spencer was a member and loved Players. I'll do it."

I asked Ray if he had any regrets. He replied, "There are a few, but mostly how so many of my portraits in print barely resemble the original—the colors are not faithful, the image has been cropped to fit the page. But I've been so fortunate to make my living in doing what I so enjoy."

EUGENE O'NEILL'S MONTE CRISTO COTTAGE

It stands back from the street, viewed from the broad expanse of lawn, and overlooks the New London Harbor. The core of the house was built around 1840. It was purchased by the actor James O'Neill in 1886 and used as rental property until 1900, when he and his family moved from their summer cottage at 134 Pequot Avenue to this house at 138 Pequot Avenue, today known as the Monte Cristo Cottage. (Around 1905, the street was renumbered, and 138 became 325 Pequot Avenue.) In preparation for moving to this cottage, O'Neill made several changes to the house. He added the turret bedroom on the second floor, French doors to draw in the morning sun, a spacious wraparound porch, raised ceilings in the first-floor rooms to impress visitors (which resulted in the upstairs bedrooms feeling cramped and small) and indoor plumbing. The living room was a one-room schoolhouse that James O'Neill moved from another location and attached to the house. To save the expense of a proper foundation, he had the building made level with the existing cottage by shoring it up on a tree trunk.

James O'Neill was a popular actor of the day. His signature role was that of Edmund Dantes in the play *The Count of Monte Cristo*. From 1900 to 1920, James O'Neill; his wife, Ella; and their children summered at the cottage. James and Ella's son Eugene Gladstone O'Neill was born in New York City on October 16, 1888. He attended Betts Academy in Stamford, and in 1906–7 he attended Princeton. He married Kathleen Jenkins in 1909 and traveled to Honduras in search of gold; in 1910, a son, Eugene Gladstone O'Neill Jr., was born. Eugene and Kathleen divorced in 1912,

The Monte Cristo Cottage, Eugene O'Neill's boyhood summer home in New London.

and he worked for the *New London Telegraph*, published poetry and entered a tuberculosis sanatorium for a six-month stay. In 1913, his first plays—*A Wife for Life* and *The Web*—were copyrighted. More plays, marriages and children followed. In 1920, *Beyond the Horizon* won the Pulitzer Prize. In 1921, *Gold*, *The Straw* and *Anna Christie* were produced. *Anna Christie* won him the Pulitzer Prize in 1921, as did *Strange Interlude* in 1928. Other plays included *The Hairy Ape*; *Mourning Becomes Electra*; *Ah, Wilderness*; *The Iceman Cometh*; and *A Moon for the Misbegotten*. In 1936, O'Neill won the Nobel Prize for Literature, the only American to be so honored. In 1953, O'Neill developed pneumonia and died on November 27.

The Monte Cristo Cottage would be important as the summer home of Eugene O'Neill. What makes it a landmark is that this is where O'Neill set his plays *Ah, Wilderness* and *A Long Day's Journey into Night*. *A Long Day's Journey into Night* is considered to be his masterpiece. In 1941, on the twelfth wedding anniversary to his wife Carlotta, he gave her the original script of *A Long Day's Journey into Night*, noting that it was a play "of old sorrow, written in tears and blood…I mean it as a tribute to your love and tenderness which gave me the faith in love that enabled me to face my death at last and write this play—with deep pity and understanding and forgiveness for all the four haunted Tyrones. These twelve years, Beloved One, have been a Journey into Light—into love."

A Long Day's Journey into Night, as Doris V. Falk, professor emeritus of English at Rutgers University, observed, was "O'Neill's own family, and their story was torn from the depths of his consciousness. With an effort compounded of 'tears and blood,' O'Neill forced himself to examine them honestly and objectively, from their own points of view as well as his." In the play, O'Neill sets the scene and meticulously describes the exterior and interior of the Monte Cristo Cottage, where he spent so many summers as a boy with his family:

> *SCENE—Living room of James Tyrone's summer home on a morning in August, 1912…At the rear are two double doorways with portieres. The one at right leads into a front parlor with the formally arranged, set appearance of a room rarely occupied…In the right wall, rear, is a screen door leading out of the porch, which extends halfway around the house. Farther forward, a series of three windows looks over the front lawn to the harbor and the avenue that runs along the water front…In the left wall, a similar series of windows look out on the grounds in back of the house. Beneath them is a wicker couch with cushions…Farther back is a large glassed-in bookcase with sets of Dumas, Victor Hugo…*

Mary Cavan Tyrone, James's wife, has some of the most haunting lines in the play, especially when talking about the cottage and the family:

> *I've never felt it was my home. It was wrong from the start. Everything was done in the cheapest way. Your father would never spend the money to make it right. It's just as well we haven't any friends here. I'd be ashamed to have them step in the door. But he's never wanted family friends…You've never had a chance to meet decent people here. I know you both would have been so different if you'd been able to associate with nice girls instead of—You'd never have disgraced yourselves as you have, so that no respectable parents will let their daughters be seen with you.*

O'Neill's manuscript of the play is dated 1940. He allowed a few close friends to read it but would not let it to be produced until twenty-five years after his death. His reason: "There is one person in it who is still alive." Some three years after his death, his wife gave the American and Canadian

The interior of the cottage that was the setting for *A Long Day's Journey into Night*; windows look over the yard, and "beneath them is a wicker couch with cushions…Farther back is a large glassed-in bookcase with sets of Dumas, Victor Hugo…"

publication rights to the Yale University Library with the stipulation that all royalties be used to establish an endowed Eugene O'Neill Memorial Fund.

The Monte Cristo Cottage was made a National Historic Landmark in 1971, owned and operated by the Eugene O'Neill Theater Center. The cottage is open to the public seasonally. Even off-season, it is a compelling, powerful and evocative place. As one walks up the long sidewalk, onto the porch and quietly peers in the windows, one expects to have one of the Tyrones come 'round the corner from an inner room. Few landmarks have that kind of presence. Even on a bright sunny day, the cottage has a moving darkness about it.

REVEREND FRANCIS GOODWIN

Transformer of a City

Mark Twain, in *A Connecticut Yankee in King Arthur's Court*, had Hank Morgan referred to as "Sir Boss." The same might have been the name given to the Reverend Francis Goodwin. Born in Hartford on September 25, 1839, he was the son of James Goodwin, a member of the very wealthy Goodwin family that was one of the founders of Hartford. Educated at home and at the Hartford Public High School, at the age of fifteen he was apprenticed to Howe, Mather & Co., dry goods merchants, and later to Morton & Grinnell of New York. He entered Berkeley Divinity School and, on May 27, 1863, was ordained a deacon in the Protestant Episcopal Church. In December, he was ordained a priest. He served as the rector of Trinity Church in Hartford from 1865 to 1871. He would from time to time assist in the running of various churches, including St. John's in Hartford, Trinity Church in Wethersfield and the Church of the Good Shepherd in Hartford and for ten years was the first archdeacon of Hartford.

Francis Goodwin's two great interests were the management of his family's wealth and the development of Hartford as a cultural and amenable city. He had a great interest in design and the English aesthetic movement and was, by his own declaration, an "amateur architect." With his brother James Junius Goodwin, he helped develop various properties, such as the Goodwin Building in Hartford at the corner of Pearl, Haynes and Asylum Streets. The Goodwin Building, built in 1881, formally recorded as designed by architects Kimball and Wisedell, is distinctive as more closely allied to

Reverend Dr. Francis Goodwin, by Charles Noel Flagg, 1911. *Wadsworth Atheneum.*

buildings being built in England at that time. The terra cotta ornaments were imported from England.

In 1868, Reverend Francis Goodwin designed his own home at 103 Woodland Street in the west end of Hartford. Four years later, according to Philip Goodwin in *Rooftrees or the Architectural History of an American Family*:

A. T. Stewart built his mansion to show what a successful dry-good merchant could do, and James Goodwin in his more modest neighborhood was urged by his enthusiastic amateur architect son [Francis] *to "tell the world" what a prosperous Hartford business man could do in his own way. But the world wags along in very regular strides, Strozzis and Medicis, Valois and Bourbons, Sackvilles and Cecils, Astors and Vanderbilts, all go about it in much the same manner. The frog is about the same, no matter what the size of the pool. So we come to James Goodwin and his son Francis, urging father to be a sport—give him a chance—spend some of his money—ad lib., until father gave in and with the help of an expert Gothicist, Mr. F. Withers, plunged into the fascinating interest of the moment.*

The house, formally known as Woodlands but locally as the Goodwin Castle, completed in 1871, was of gray granite, banded with pink, some 275 feet across, not including the greenhouses, icehouse, stables, et cetera. It was all surrounded by "a light iron railing, painted in red, picked out here and there with black and gold." Inside, Francis selected the most modern wallpapers, including ones by William Morris and others. One was of brilliantly colored birds on a black background. The house had five bathrooms, was lit by gas and though it was wired for electricity in 1891, it was "never used. It was considered dangerous."

Reverend Francis Goodwin served as a trustee of Trinity College, the Watkinson Library (now at Trinity College) and the Watkinson School; was on the Board of Street Commissioners; was director of the Institute of Living; was president of the Wadsworth Atheneum; and was a member of the Hartford Park Commissioners. As the head of the Wadsworth Atheneum, he persuaded his cousin J.P. Morgan to buy the land south of the existing building and to erect the Morgan Memorial in honor of his father, Junius Morgan. Later, Goodwin would direct that the land next to the museum, at the corner of Main and Arch Streets "should be used for the building of a new Municipal Building" (city hall) for Hartford. It was completed in 1915. When the 1879 committee to honor the memory of the soldiers and sailors who had died in the Civil War had accomplished absolutely nothing, Reverend Goodwin stepped in. In 1881, he had the committee reappointed, had Colonel George Bissell made the chair and, on December 6, 1881, according to the minutes of the committee, had the committee select Bushnell Park as the site for the memorial. He directed that they should "take into consideration the feasibility of constructing a bridge combined with an emblematic Arch…Mr. Goodwin exhibited a sketch or

At Goodwin's request, his cousin J.P. Morgan donated the funds to purchase the land and build this addition to the Wadsworth Atheneum. It is known as the Morgan Memorial in honor of his father, Hartford native Junius Spencer Morgan.

study of such a work, with plan, side and front elevations, drawn by Mr. Withers, Architect." It is known today as the Soldiers' and Sailors' Memorial Arch in Bushnell Park.

As the first Hartford parks commissioner, he was singularly responsible for what would be known as "the rain of parks." He championed green spaces for the city; his slogan was "More Parks for Hartford." Hartford had just two parks at the time: South Green (1821) in Hartford, at the intersection of Main Street and Wethersfield Avenue (Park Street is named for the small park), and Bushnell Park (1854). Goodwin believed that the city should be encircled with parks. Goodwin is said to have consoled Charles M. Pond after the death of his wife, Elizabeth, and persuaded him to leave his one-hundred-acre estate to Hartford. He convinced Colonel Albert A. Pope to donate a ninety-acre tract to become a park. Working as a trustee under the will of Henry Keney (a relative by marriage), he directed architect Charles Haight in the design of the Keney Memorial Clock Tower, which is today on the small parklet on North Main Street. Goodwin engineered, under Keney's will, the purchase of land parcels that would become Keney Park on the northern border of Hartford. The sum allotted for the park was $100,000. Designed by Olmsted Brothers, when the park was officially deeded to the city, because of Goodwin's shrewd investments and careful management, the city received the deed for the land and a check for $100,000.

Riverside Park was added under Goodwin's tenure. In 1900, Skinner's Woods, 237 acres in the south end in Hartford and Wethersfield, was acquired. It completed Goodwin's dream of a park system that encircled the city, making parks accessible to all. In 1901, it was named in his honor: Goodwin Park.

Said at the time to be "recognized as Hartford's largest individual tax payer," it must be noted that where he had influence, resources and connections, for all the smiling benevolence portrayed in photographs and portraits, Goodwin could be a very tough and exacting individual. He was a focused and persuasive businessman. When Goodwin was developing the west end of his family's land between Woodland Street and Prospect Avenue, in his May 10, 1880 petition he asked that a new city road be constructed to connect Albany Avenue and Asylum Street and said, "It is proposed to call the new street Scarborough Street—Miss Janet and Luther Scarborough were sixty years and more ago, prominent citizens of Hartford, & the former was a large owner of land in this vicinity. Prospect Hill was then and long afterward known as Scarborough Hill." In all the city records and directories, there is no record of a Janet or Luther Scarborough. With the phrase "sixty years and more ago," one suspects the reverend wished to name it after Scarborough, England, and wrapped his desire in a cloak of sentiment of individuals gone before anyone could recall so he could get his way.

Not everyone endorsed the doings of Reverend Francis Goodwin. In 1910, James Terry of Wethersfield Avenue issued a broadside titled "SHALL THE CITY OF HARTFORD AND STATE OF CONNECTICUT BE DOMINATED BY THE PATERNALISM OF REV. FRANCIS GOODWIN?" The motive for the piece is not known, but the writer presented an open challenge to the "insider-connections" amongst the members of the Goodwin family and their associates, friends and relations. It is clear that the Hartford that one knows today would not be the city that it is had it not been guided, shaped, influenced and directed by the Reverend Francis Goodwin.

CEDAR HILL CEMETERY

Every spring, after a seemingly endless winter, I, for one, am filled with the desire to get out, to walk and to enjoy the warm air and flowering plants, shrubs and trees. I find that the quintessential place to do this is at the sprawling 270-acre Cedar Hill Cemetery. Located on Hartford's southern border with Wethersfield, at the junction of Maple Avenue and Fairfield Avenue, Cedar Hill is a wonder.

A cemetery? Am I seriously recommending a graveyard as a place to go for a stroll? Yes. Cedar Hill is also a great destination for explorers, adventurers, history buffs or kids. Cemeteries are often thought of as barren fields of granite stones set in rows, somber and negative. Beautifully landscaped and meticulously maintained, Cedar Hill is different from the rest. It is a sculpture garden of fantastic monuments—big and small, full of extraordinary carvings, finely sculptured or severely plain and carefully polished. They note the greats and the near greats who have passed before us. The combination of a carefully manipulated landscape framed by a wide range of trees and bushes provides one with a panorama that is more than memorable. Despite the solemn reason for Cedar Hill, one feels a sense of joy and renewal when visiting. It is like no other cemetery in its sheer beauty.

Founded in 1864, Cedar Hill was designed to provide peace and harmony for the Victorians who "rested" within its grounds, as well as for those who came to visit them. It was designed by Jacob Weidenmann, who also designed Bushnell Park. There are two ways to plan your visit to Cedar Hill. One is to have the Cedar Hill office send you one of its detailed tour guides.

You can call the office at 860-965-3311 to request one or visit the website: cedarhillcemetery.org. The other is to just go and discover.

Cedar Hill's landscape, as designed by Weidenmann, is breathtaking. You enter through formal stone gates. On the immediate left is the Northam Memorial Chapel, which was designed by architect George Keller in 1882. No longer used as a chapel, in 1999 it was restored and today serves as the cemetery's business offices. Proceed west down a long drive. On the left is Llyn Mawr, meaning "Great Lake." It creates a sense of serenity and peace, and serves to separate you from the traffic and the busy world you have just left. The road rises slightly as you enter the formal grounds. Because of the careful manipulation of the landscape, you can take in only small vistas at a time. At the flagpole, take the lower left road; it is time to park the car and go exploring.

Near the road, you will see a monument to Horace Wells (1815–1848), the Hartford dentist who discovered anesthesia. His grave has a most curious bas-relief plaque by Louis Potter. It shows a half-reclining figure in great pain being administered to by the spirit of anesthesia. The spirit has a potion to relieve the suffering. Below the scene are the words: "They shall feel no pain." Wells used nitrous oxide, or laughing gas, for his anesthesia and is said to have experimented extensively on himself. Under the influence, he became a true Jekyll and Hyde and would go out and strangle young prostitutes. He died at the young age of thirty-three.

Once you pass the Terry Cross, take the first road to the right. On the left, in Section 3, will be the Welles family plot. On March 6, 1860, Abraham Lincoln, who had spoken in Hartford the day before, came to the Brown and Gross bookstore on the corner of Main and Asylum Streets. There he met with Gideon Welles (1802–1878). They had a two-hour discussion on politics and economics, which led to Welles's appointment as Lincoln's secretary of the navy. The Welles family were prominent in Glastonbury.

Continue along the road and at the intersection take a right to Section 4. About midway you will see the Hooker plot. Descended from Hartford's founder, the Reverend Thomas Hooker, John Hooker (1816–1901) was a respected lawyer. His wife, Isabella Beecher Hooker (1822–1907), was the sister of popular nineteenth-century preacher Henry Ward Beecher and half-sister of Harriet Beecher Stowe. Isabella was a noted suffragette. She was also outspoken, worked tirelessly for women's rights and believed in mediums and spiritualists. She was probably the most interesting woman who ever lived in this state. Her grave is marked with a simple seventeenth-century table-type monument evoking earlier ancestors and is totally non-reflective of who rests beneath.

If one climbs the hill behind and ascends to the highest point (Section 2), he will see a great pink granite monument with Egyptian motifs. This is the grave of Colonel Sam Colt (1814–1862); his wife, Elizabeth (1826–1905); and their children. Colt was a Hartford boy whose revolver changed the world. "God created man equal; Sam Colt made them so" was the slogan of the day. The Colt Factory building in Hartford survives, and there are plans to establish the factory area as a national park. Sam Colt and the three children who died in infancy were originally buried on his Hartford estate Armsmear, on "the sacred acre." After their sole surviving child Caldwell died of curious circumstances at the age of thirty-six in 1894, Mrs. Colt began to put her affairs in order. She arranged for the bodies of her husband and their children to be moved from Armsmear and reinterred on the highest point in Cedar Hill. She commissioned J. Massey Rhind, a sculptor in New York, to create the suitable monument to her husband at Armsmear on the site of the sacred acre. In her will, she left the house to the Episcopal Diocese of Connecticut for "widows or orphans of deceased [Episcopal] clergymen" and "impoverished but refined and educated gentlewomen." The rest of the estate's acreage she left to the City of Hartford for a park.

As you explore the ridge, you will soon discover many prominent Victorians. Among them are Bishop Thomas Church Brownell (1799–1865) and Pliny Jewell (1797–1869). Right Reverend Brownell was the Episcopal bishop of Connecticut, the presiding bishop of the Episcopal Church in America and the first president of Trinity College. Pliny Jewell manufactured superior leather belting used in factories, including Colt's. In his retirement, Pliny liked to train and feed the frogs in Elizabeth Park. (Note to history buffs: in Hartford, "Pliny" rhymes with "slimy," while in Boston it rhymes with "skinny.")

Colonel Sam Colt's monument at Cedar Hill Cemetery is the tallest monument on the tallest hill. One would expect nothing less.

Proceed to the south, cross the road and walk to the middle of Section 3. Morgan Gardner Bulkeley (1837–1922) was the president of the Aetna Insurance Co. and at the same time served as Hartford's mayor (1880–88), Connecticut's governor (1889–93) and U.S. senator (1905–11). Though his political aspirations to become president of the United States were not realized, he was the first president of baseball's National League and is in the Baseball Hall of Fame in Cooperstown, New York. He also led the drive that saved the Old State House from demolition in 1917.

Now proceed to the west along the road that runs between Sections 1 and 2. On the way, you will pass a monument to Dr. Cincinnatus Taft (1822–1884), Mark Twain's doctor. Proceed along the road and up the hill to Section 11. At the top of the hill on the left is a large rose-colored granite monument in the shape of the Arc of the Covenant. This marks the grave of John Pierpont Morgan (1837–1913) and his family. A Hartford native, J.P. Morgan was born at 159 Asylum Street, where City Place now stands. He was once the richest and most powerful man in America.

Head to the north and cross the road into Section 10. Here one will find monuments to the Goodwin family, Hartford founders and leaders of the community. The Reverend Francis Goodwin (1839–1923) developed the Hartford park system and transformed Hartford in the early part of the twentieth century. Benjamin Wistar Morris (1870–1944) was the noted architect who designed the state armory and the Avery Wing of the Wadsworth Atheneum. Because he married a Goodwin, he is buried in Cedar Hill. One will also find James Goodwin Batterson (1823–1901) in this section. He managed the New England Granite Works that built the Connecticut State Capitol and the Library of Congress in Washington. He did his own translations of Homer's *Iliad* and *Odyssey*, and in 1864 he founded the Travelers Insurance Co. to insure people when traveling. George Capewell (1843–1919), who developed the machine that mass-produced horseshoe nails, is here as well. His grave, as you might expect, is ornamented with horseshoes and nails. Here also are Henry (1806–1894) and Walter (1808–1889) Keney. After his brother's death, Henry Keney drew up his will. He left considerable sums to a variety of institutions in the city. On the site of their homestead, he directed that the house be razed, lest it fall into misuse, and in its place a tower be erected as a memorial to their mother. Keney's father died when he and his brother were young, but their mother kept the grocery business growing until they were old enough to run it. The tower was the first monument in America erected to a woman, simply because she was their mother. Keney also left the funds to acquire the

The Hepburn family plot is marked by a simple boulder. The actress's grave site is just in front of it, marked by a simple flat headstone.

land on the northern part of the city to create a park that would bear their name: Keney Park.

These are but a few of the highlights you will find as you stroll Weidenman's carefully designed "sculpture" park. More luminaries to be found here include Gilbert Heublein (1849–1937) of A-1 Sauce fame and importer of Smirnoff vodka; Thomas Gallaudet (1787–1851) of the American School for the Deaf; Reverend Joseph Twitchell (1838–1918), Mark Twain's minister and the pastor of Asylum Hill Congregational Church; Colonel Albert Pope (1843–1909), who manufactured the Columbia bicycle and the Pope automobile; and the star of stage and screen "local girl" Katharine Hepburn (1907–2003), who to date has won more Oscars (four) than any other actress. Others buried here have names that may have been totally forgotten but whose monuments, or the trees that shelter them, continue to provide visual pleasure and interest.

When your journey is over, drop into the First and Last Tavern just down the hill on Maple Avenue for some bodily refreshment.

THE CURIOUS MONUMENT ON AVON MOUNTAIN

T alcott Mountain is the name given to the thirteen-mile ridge of trap rock that makes up the Metacomet Ridge, which extends from Long Island Sound near New Haven through the Connecticut River Valley and on to the Vermont border. The section crossed by Albany Avenue, U.S. 44, west of West Hartford is locally known as Avon Mountain. When one is driving west on Albany Avenue and crosses the summit of the ridge, then begins the descent into Avon, on the western edge there is suddenly a curious monument. Comprising six tapered Quincy polished gray granite blocks, its base is seventy-six feet across the face, thirty-one feet deep and stands over twelve feet high. Above the center is a three-foot bronze medallion with a portrait head of a man in bas-relief. It is encircled with the inscription: "Pioneer of Highways—James Henry MacDonald." Hundreds drive by the monument daily. Who was MacDonald, and why was the monument placed there?

James MacDonald was born in New Haven in 1851. In 1895, he was appointed to the state's original highway commission. In 1897, he became Connecticut's first one-man commission, a post he held until 1913. The *New Haven Journal-Courier* reported in 1933 that he was "one of the first national prophets of the present automobile era. His services began when the gas-buggy was only a dare-devil's plaything, when Henry Ford was tinkering with bicycles, when the carriage-driver used to climb out and turn away his steed's head as one of the snorting, fuming, clanking monsters exploded past."

MacDonald established the original trunk roads that ran through every town in the state. He advocated before town meetings that good roads were essential to the growth and prosperity of the state. Commissioner John A. Macdonald remembered that James H. MacDonald was "a pioneer of highways in this and many other states. I recall as a boy seeing him drive his Pope-Hartford car through my town, officially known as 'The Pioneer' but more affectionately as 'Betsy,' and after having been driven over 100,000 miles, finally burned up in the vicinity of Barkhamsted."

In 1931, the state established a James H. MacDonald Memorial Commission to erect a suitable tablet "in commemoration of the engineering achievements of James H. MacDonald, former state highway commissioner, as a pioneer in the development of highways." The five-acre site on Avon Mountain was purchased from Joseph W. Alsop. It was selected as MacDonald considered the development of that stretch of road to be one of his "most important achievements." According to the *Hartford Courant*, he saw the section as an "open door" over Avon Mountain to northwestern Connecticut, the Berkshires and New York State. Before it was improved by Commissioner MacDonald, the road had a 25 percent grade in sections that could be surmounted only with the greatest difficulty. He personally reviewed the terrain and chose the places where the most grade changes could be achieved for the lowest cost. He had the highway blasted out of solid rock to a width of thirty-two feet, for some one thousand feet in length, and the 25 percent grade was greatly reduced. According to the press, "The job was done for less than $250,000 and caused engineers from other states to marvel at the accomplishment of such a feat at low cost."

On the afternoon of Wednesday, August 30, 1933, before an assembled crowd of nearly one thousand,

The James H. MacDonald Monument on Avon Mountain, U.S. 44.

Connecticut governor Wilbur Cross unveiled the monument and memorial medallion. The governor paid tribute to MacDonald, who "brought science into road building and fought to redeem dirt roads from the thraldom of mud." The governor added that it was MacDonald who had persuaded the General Assembly to adopt the policy of state aid to towns. MacDonald died on September 23, 1938. After his death, someone added to the monument just below the medallion his dates: 1851–1938.

It should be noted that the medallion plaque was sculpted by Evelyn Longman. She is one of America's foremost sculptors. She won the blind competition for the bronze doors of the U.S. Naval Academy's chapel at Annapolis, was chosen to sculpt the *Spirit of Electricity* figure that once topped the AT&T Building in New York City, did all the lettering and decorative elements for French at the Lincoln Memorial and worked on numerous other commissions. In 1920, she married Nathaniel Batchelder, the founding headmaster of the Loomis Institute, now Loomis Chafee School in Windsor, Connecticut. In 1919, she was the first female sculptor elected to full membership in the National Academy of Design.

So the next time one is driving the Albany Turnpike on Avon Mountain, going from "hither to yon," look for the MacDonald monument and thank him. Without his pioneering vision that roads were the future and his engineering skills, one just might not make the grade.

ADAM VAN DOREN

An Artist's Journey

H is ancestors came to New Jersey in the seventeenth century. His grandfather Mark taught at Columbia University and was one of its most legendary professors. Among his students were John Berryman, Lionel Trilling and Whittaker Chambers. Jack Kerouac quit the football team to spend more time studying Shakespeare with him. He helped keep Alan Ginsberg out of jail by testifying on his behalf. Adam's great-uncle Carl, also a Columbia professor, wrote *The American Novel*, which is credited with reestablishing Melville's critical status as a literary master. His father, John, was the editor of *Encyclopedia Britannica's* annual *Great Ideas Today*. His grandmother Dorothy was a novelist, and his great-aunt Irita was once described as one of New York's "leading literary figures." Adam's mother, the painter Mira Jewabnik, exposed him to the world of easels and pigments and the smell of paint. In a family dominated by writers and scholars, Adam had a natural talent and love of drawing and painting. At six, he began drawing cartoons and a comic strip, *Adam's People*. At eleven, he had an agent and a small business in greeting cards. He took watercolor classes at Chicago's Artists Guild and oil painting classes at the Art Institute. At eighteen, his paintings were exhibited at the Art Institute. Where art school would have seemed the logical place after high school, Adam elected to go to Columbia. He saw the importance of the well-rounded liberal arts education, Columbia's core curriculum, and appreciated the New York arts scene.

At Columbia, Adam took postmodern architect Robert A.M. Stern's undergraduate course. Stern believed in a very traditional approach, insisting that the students master the fundamentals of architecture, including the basic visual vocabulary of Classical architecture. Students were required to learn to draw in traditional ways and then to paint them in the Beaux-Arts technique, doing the renderings in watercolor—a multitude of washes, sometimes twenty or more. Where Adam had an incredible talent for drawing, he mastered the art of watercolor renderings and remarked, "I never looked at buildings the same way again." He graduated from Columbia and later from its architecture school and apprenticed with architectural firms.

But his heart wasn't in being an architect in the traditional sense. He had a passion for the beauty of structure and detail. He came across Christopher Alexander's *A Pattern Language* in which the architect believed that the user, not the architect, should be in charge of designing a space or a building. This was outside the discipline of architecture. Adam "longed for something real." He wanted to get his hands dirty. With the help of craftsmen, he restored the overshot waterwheel in the mill on his property in western Connecticut. He switched from architecture to painting. Having always had a natural talent for drawing, he developed the skill of an accomplished but traditional watercolor artist, and his works were well received. He exhibited both nationally and internationally, including at the National Portrait Gallery in Washington, D.C.; at the University of Venice; and at the Chicago Institute of Fine Arts and is in the permanent collections of the Wadsworth Atheneum; the New Britain Museum of American Art; the Museum of Fine Arts, Houston; and the Art Institute of Chicago, among others.

His watercolors were very good and received most favorable mention. There was an understandable concentration on buildings and design elements. In New York, he joined a painting group. Among the artists were David Levine, best known for his caricatures in the *New York Review of Books*, and Aaron Shikler, whose works include the official White House portraits of President Kennedy and Mrs. Kennedy. Here he was exposed to rapid-fire conversations, other artists, galleries, commissions and art directors. He traveled to Rome, Venice and Paris. A plein air artist, he continued to paint in a classic manner, but he was becoming restless. The more he painted, the more he began to look for a less-controlled approach, a greater freedom of expression. In the back of his mind, he kept hearing the voice of a former teacher in a painting class: "We all know that Adam is great at drawing. That is not required for painting. Painting is about color." If Adam had continued to paint in that tight, restricted manner, one would not be reading about him here.

In 2011, Adam went to MOMA's exhibit "German Expressionism: The Graphic Impulse." Adam was especially struck by the watercolors of Emil

Above: Adam Van Doren's watercolor *Yellow Sky*, 2011, marks his free departure into the future.

Right: Adam Van Doren in his Connecticut home.

Nolde: "Nolde lets watercolor take on vibrancy; it bleeds and flows and is improvisational. He has freed up the artist. I found his breaking of the traditional structure liberating."

Suddenly, Adam went in a whole new direction. His watercolors are now on a large scale, the paper twenty-four inches wide or more. He paints with different tools—charcoal, not pencil—and he prefers the vibrancy and freedom a charcoal line presents when infused with color. "In larger spaces, I needed the materials to sweep the distance," he said. His architectural detailed elements are now replaced by vast landscapes of incredible color and energy. *Yellow Sky* is a watercolor on paper, twenty-one by thirty inches. It was painted in 2011. The rich landscape in the foreground, the streaked and reflective water and the vibrant yellow sky hold it together with freedom and movement.

His lineage was one of scholarship and structure. Adam is now his own man. "What is past, is prologue" (Shakespeare, *The Tempest*). He has found the freedom to chart new courses, with compelling and moving results. His artistic journey has just begun. One looks forward to the works that Adam will create on that journey.

BUSHNELL PARK

Setting the Record Straight

You have probably read or heard many times that 1) Bushnell Park in Hartford was set aside to be a fresh-air space for kids from the slums, the Front Street area, et cetera; 2) that it was designed by America's foremost landscape architect Frederick Law Olmsted; 3) that it was a dump before Reverend Horace Bushnell rescued it; and 4) that the statues on the base of the arch were carved by Albert Entress. For the record, all of the above statements are just not true. Yet even today, the print, radio, TV and social media; books such as Sterner's inaccurate *A Guide to Historic Hartford*; and even the foundation that has admirably protected and enhanced the park, cling to and continue to spread these myths. One can speculate whether it is laziness, wishful thinking or the hope that if it is repeated enough it might become the truth. Here is the history of Bushnell Park, based on documents, contemporary council minutes, periodicals and account books and not wishful thinking.

1) Bushnell Park comprises some thirty-five acres in the center of the city of Hartford, through which the Little River, today known as the Park River, once flowed. Trinity College was originally located on the southern edge of the area, the site today occupied by the present state capitol. It is always romantic to think that Hartford businessmen in the mid-nineteenth century wanted an open-air park for all the city's citizens. The reality and customs of the time present a different picture. The slums of Hartford, the low-lying areas near the Connecticut River, were where the poorest lived. The area flooded in the spring and fall. The conditions were terrible. Eighteen wharfs

composed the Port of Hartford. It was a slum, filled with poverty, prostitution, disease, et cetera. Anyone who saw the film *Gangs of New York* saw the culture of that time around the docks and waterfront. Those who lived there would not have been allowed to cross Market Street, let alone Main Street. Those who might avail themselves of a carriage ride in Bushnell Park would not have tolerated having their rides crossed by "street urchins." One needs to be careful not to impose twenty-first-century views on earlier times. The notion of reserving prime land for a park out of humanitarian generosity was never the motive behind Bushnell Park. It was a business decision.

On October 5, 1853, Reverend Horace Bushnell, of the Fourth Congregational Church, addressed a meeting of the city's court of common council proposing a plan for a park. A committee was formed consisting of Messrs. Robinson, Howard, Bolter, Wright, Merritt and Danforth to study the idea. In Bushnell's testimony, as reported in the *Hartford Courant* (October 7, 1853), he stated that the park should be interior, within the city limits, and "it should be a spot where, if necessary the State House might be erected. There are many objections to the present location of

Bushnell Park was proposed in 1853 as the site of the new capitol building when the state made Hartford the sole capital.

the State House [today known as the Old State House at 800 Main Street in Hartford]. It may become necessary soon to erect a new one. He would therefore have the site of the Park so chosen that it would prove the very best spot for a new State House."

Following the joining of the colony of Connecticut and the colony of New Haven into one colony, the state had two capitals. The legislature would meet in New Haven in the fall and in Hartford in the spring. By the 1850s, this moving of the legislature and courts every six months was becoming an unwieldy and expensive process.

Bushnell did make the opening statement, but the real manager of securing the area called Central Park, today known as Bushnell Park, was Colonel James E. Bolter. He was a Hartford businessman, wholesale grocer, bank cashier and later president of the Hartford Bank. He was on various bank and insurance boards and served on the Hartford Court of Common Council, the board of aldermen and the board of the water commissioners. Where Bushnell is not present and is not mentioned in any of the subsequent proceedings, Bolter is never absent. Every process, especially one that would remove some thirty-five acres from the tax rolls, needed to be efficiently and carefully managed. Bolter was that manager, right down to selecting the date when the citizens of Hartford would vote to approve or reject the park. The date was January 5, 1854. It passed, 1,005 to 682.

From the very beginning, it is clear that the idea of the park was simply a business decision. It was a business strategy to have a local minister introduce the idea. The idea for creating this central park was that when the two-capital arrangement became too burdensome, Hartford would have a site all dressed up and ready to serve. All of the initial landscape plans and testimony make open reference that this should be the site for the new capitol building. On May 21, 1870, the citizens of Hartford voted that if the state declared Hartford the sole capital, the city would commit $500,000 toward the new building in the park. At his inauguration as governor on May 16, 1871, Marshall Jewell from Hartford stated that he would propose legislation to have only one capital. After many maneuvers, in July 1871, the bill on authorizing the new capitol in Hartford, the issuance of "capitol bonds" and the appointment of a building committee passed. The committee first met on August 25, 1871. On April 18, 1872, the second competition for the design of the new capitol was held; it was won by Richard M. Upjohn. After many objections and politicking, referendums and objections, on May 5, 1875, Hartford became the sole capital. The legislature met in Hartford, in the Old State House, and no longer in New Haven.

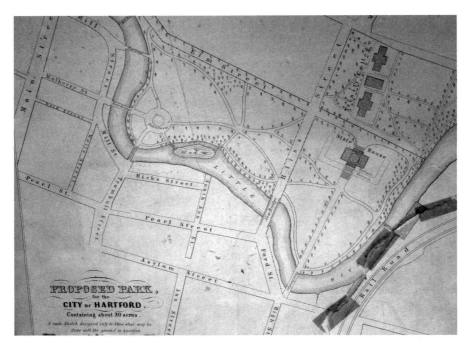

Seth Marsh's original 1858 pen-and-ink plan. It shows the proposed location for the "new" State House on the right. *Hartford Town/City Archives, Hartford History Center.*

2) After the citizens of Hartford voted for the park, then known as Central Park, there was a great deal of work that needed to be undertaken. The city took possession of the few structures that dotted the landscape, and in 1858 the Central Park Committee held a competition for the best working plan for the park. The *Hartford Daily Times*, on June 3, 1858, reported that "it is suggested that Frederick Law Olmsted, a native of this city, who has lately been chosen to superintend the laying out of the large park in New York, would be a proper person to give shape to the result of our more modest enterprise." There is no record or evidence in any of the newspapers, parks reports or even the Olmsted papers that Olmsted responded to the request, if indeed it was ever made. He had nothing to do with the park. A Mr. Wheeler of New York won the competition, but his proposal was apparently too expensive. The city selected the second prizewinner Seth Marsh of Hartford's plan as a start.

The early work focused on draining the low areas and making other improvements and seems to have happened in fits and starts. Because of the lack of progress on May 28, 1860, the city established the Hartford

Board of Parks Commissioners. On July 17, 1860, the board hired Jacob Weidenmann as the first superintendent of the park. Born in Switzerland, he was formally trained in drawing, engineering and architecture. According to Weidenmann scholar Rudy Favretti, his first task was to make "accurate surveys and plans for drainage and to lay out the ground, with a working plan showing all the walks, planting and other improvements." Weidenmann later was the landscape designer of Cedar Hill Cemetery. He urged the establishment of a professional school to raise landscape architecture to a proper standing. Harvard University awards the Jacob Weidenmann prize to the student who has shown outstanding ability in landscape design. Some have stated that Olmsted recommended Weidenmann for the job. Olmsted's biographer Laura Wood Roper found no documented relationship between Olmsted and Weidenmann, or Olmsted and the Hartford park, and stated that they did not even meet until 1862.

3) The concept that Bushnell Park was a dump is one fabricated and promoted by the Reverend Horace Bushnell himself. Ralph Earl's portrait of Colonel Samuel Talcott, 1791, and Joseph Ropes's painting of *View of Hartford to the West, 1855,* both in the collection of the Wadsworth Atheneum, as well as sketches by Frederic Church at Olana, show the acreage as one of open lawns; a few houses, such as the Bliss House; a few dams; and little else. There was a gristmill and a flour mill and an icehouse. Other images depict people fishing beside the river. In 1833, a brownstone bridge was built over the Little River at Main Street, connecting the northern and southern parts of the city. In 1838, a modest single rail line was run through the area to a passenger depot at Mulberry Street, today near the corner of Trumbull and Gold Streets. (It was removed in 1856.) On December 14, 1839, the first train came into Hartford, connecting the city with Springfield, Meriden, New Haven and New York. In 1849, a main train station, an elaborate Italianate depot, was built northwest of the area at Asylum Street and Spruce Street, where the present Hartford station is located.

In the February 6, 1869 issue of *Hearth and Home* some sixteen years after his appearance before the city council, Bushnell wrote that the site was a desperate dump, a "hell without fire." The primarily open green space had, by 1869, been improved by Weidenmann's design, including walks and plantings. There is no record of this ever being a dump or a "hell without fire." But sixteen years later is a very, very long time for anyone to remember the "what was" when the "now" is a landscaped public park. To further take credit for what never was, Bushnell added, "Forbidding as the picture was, I saw merit and capacity in the ground, and took up in earnest the question how to obtain it."

4) In 1879, the City of Hartford established a committee to look into the cost of erecting a suitable monument to the soldiers and seamen from Hartford who died in the Civil War. In 1881, because the first commission had accomplished nothing, a new commission was established; Colonel George P. Bissell was chosen as the chairman and Sherman W. Adams as the secretary. The committee invited ideas, and the Reverend Francis Goodwin proposed that the memorial be in the form of an arch with a bridge to serve as an entrance into Bushnell Park. In May 1883, a competition was held based on Goodwin's concept, but it was determined that none could be constructed within the allowed budget. In December 1883, architect George Keller wrote to Mr. Adams that if the committee was willing to consider a new design, he had a proposal for it to consider. On December 15, 1883, he presented to the committee. By substituting local brownstone and cast terra cotta for more costly granite and marble, and by cladding the existing Ford Street Bridge instead of building a new one, the project would probably meet the budget.

On January 21, 1884, the committee accepted Keller's proposal. On May 21, 1884, the committee awarded the contracts for the memorial. Hiram Bissell was the general contractor. Samuel Kitson of New York sculpted the north frieze that told the story of war. Caspar Buberl, also of New York, sculpted the southern frieze that told the story of peace and of the arch's top two angels. The committee voted to delay the commissioning of the six statues near the base of the arch, three on each side, until a later time. The arch was dedicated on September 17, 1886, the fourteenth anniversary of the Battle of Antietam.

The account book for the arch is in the collection of the Connecticut Historical Society. On January 8, 1890, the committee voted to contract with Caspar Buberl to sculpt "six eight feet high statues" representing a farmer leaving his plow and grasping a gun; a blacksmith leaving his hammer for a cutlass; a mason with a war wound bandage picking up his trowel; a carpenter wearing his soldier's hat measuring a plan; a student in a thoughtful pose; and a slave breaking the chains of bondage with one arm while holding a slate with the alphabet in the other. (The slave statue replaced the earlier proposed one of a merchant.)

Caspar Buberl completed the commission, and the account book states that he was paid $2,544.26. What was Albert Entress's role in the arch, and why is he so often credited with Buberl's work? Entress was contracted to position the statues. Entress was a noted architectural sculptor, one often used by Keller. He sculpted the twelve pinnacles and other decorative

The Soldiers' and Sailors' Memorial Arch in Bushnell Park.

elements on Christ Church Cathedral in Hartford. He sculpted the base for the statue of Lafayette near the state capitol. There is no record of his ever carving figures. In all his advertisements and notices, he lists himself as an architectural sculptor. His task at the arch was to take Buberl's statues and

The Soldiers' and Sailors' Memorial Arch with Buberl's eight-foot-high sculpture of a mason with a war wound bandage picking up his trowel.

cut away their backs and part of the arch's finished towers to receive the figures so they would appear to be fitting into the monument without gaps. It is a task that allows for no errors and must be done by a skilled artisan. Entress was paid $1,500. So where did the attribution that Entress was the sculptor of the six statues come from? It was an attribution made by his granddaughter years later and is without merit.

The man most responsible for the establishment of the park was Bolter. The man who liked to take the credit was Bushnell. Three days before Bushnell's death, apparently at the request of his family, who were prominently connected, the Hartford Court of Common Council, on February 14, 1876, voted to rename City Park or Central Park as Bushnell Park. In 1919, his daughter Dotha Bushnell Hillyer, wife of Hartford banker Appleton R. Hillyer, began planning a great memorial to her father. The result was the construction of Bushnell Memorial Hall. Its cornerstone was laid by Dotha's daughter on October 16, 1928. The hall opened on January 13, 1930, and is today known as the Bushnell Center for the Performing Arts.

MATTATUCK MUSEUM OF WATERBURY

The Mattatuck Museum of Waterbury was established as the Mattatuck Historical Society in 1877 to preserve the history of the ten-town area surrounding and including present-day Waterbury. The Paugasuck (Paugasett) Indians were the original holders of the land and called it *Mattatuck*, "badly wooded," on both sides of the Naugatuck River. In the 1960s, the historical society broadened its mission to "collect and exhibit the works of Connecticut artists." The expanded mission was not a great change for the institution. As early as 1912, it had been exhibiting paintings by American artists. The first major exhibition displayed paintings from New York's Montross Gallery.

Today, the Mattatuck Museum continues to both preserve the history and heritage of the Naugatuck Valley and expand and serve the larger interests of the population. Its 2012 "Art for Everyone" exhibition of art created under President Roosevelt's Works Progress Administration (WPA) fostered a new appreciation and understanding of the artists and the era. In Connecticut, 173 artists produced over five thousand works. Waterbury is known as the brass city, and predictably and appropriately there are ample exhibits sharing this moniker, including the Waterbury Button Museum's holdings. Assembled by Warren F. Kaynor for the company, it has, neatly arranged, over fifteen thousand buttons from 1812 to the end of the twentieth century. The museum's permanent collection has important works by Alexander Calder, Arshile Gorky, John Frederick Kensett, Kay Sage, Yves Tanguy and John Trumbull. It has an impressive and engaging role in the community, in

The Mattatuck Museum of Waterbury.

the schools, engaging local artists and citizens and addressing their interests and needs.

The Mattatuck's exhibition "Coming Home: Building Community in a Changing World" shatters all the rules and conventions found in a museum that attempts to create an exhibition that shares the evolution of a community. Often titled "History Is All Around Us" or some similar sophomoric slogan, other exhibits bore the visitor with innocuous and totally uninformed labels and with a layout that doesn't connect or work except for those who already know the way. Mattatuck's is public history at its best. It engages the visitor without pandering or condescension. It is laid out so one can follow the chronological journey or hopscotch and wander at will; one is exploring, discovering, and one is engaged! Visually, it hits all the buttons. Decades are noted in white numbers (1890, 1900, et cetera) cut into the gray carpet. Some kids make a game of it, jumping from decade to decade and then stopping on the numbers and peering at the objects in the case. Panels note "Meet James Scoville, 1789–1857," and one has to open the panel to learn more. As one kid did this when I visited, he remarked, "Cool!" and then proceeded to engage and "meet" other people along the journey.

The exhibition does not duck some hard issues. There are sections on life in the city, life in the neighborhood and panels such as "Meet Mary O., factory worker" or John S. Monagan. Regional celebrities include Rosalind Russell, "Auntie Mame," Chief Too Moons of herbal medicine and Candy La Chance, the major-league baseball player who played for Boston in 1903.

The museum's wonderfully engaging exhibit "Coming Home: Building Community in a Changing World" is the refreshing and engaging example that such presentations can indeed be terrific. It is the only one I've seen that works. Go check it out!

In the cases are items from the collection made in the region: furniture, brass fittings for kerosene lamps, door knobs, jars, pottery, toys, clocks and fine furniture, all displayed as a celebration of Waterbury and the surrounding towns. Regardless of one's interest in art or culture, take a moment, go to Waterbury and see how a really good small museum can do it right!

YALE AND TITLE IX

In a single act, a small group of female rowers at an Ivy League college changed the course of women's athletics nationally and beyond. The Civil Rights Act of 1964 was written to end discrimination based on religion, race, color or national origin. In 1967, President Johnson sent a series of executive orders to clarify the law. Under Executive Order 11375, it required all institutions receiving federal contracts to end discrimination on the basis of sex. Senator Birch Bayh introduced Title IX as an amendment to the Higher Education Act that was under consideration for reauthorization. The act, as amended, was signed into law by President Nixon on June 23, 1972. Where many have identified Title IX as equalizing the disparity between the facilities and status of men's and women's athletic programs, that was not the case. From the beginning, many were concerned how Title IX would adversely affect men's athletics. Today, one cites Title IX as changing the landscape and equalizing, among other things, men's and women's athletics at institutions of higher learning. Nothing could be farther from the truth. That happened because of individuals such as Chris Ernst.

Yale began accepting women as undergraduates in 1969. That did not mean that women were considered equals by their male counterparts in any respect. Nowhere was this more evident than in the Athletics Department. As Carmen Cozza, Yale's legendary football coach (1965–96), remarked, "To the men, the women had invaded their turf." Yale considered women's athletics as club or intramural programs, giving them little support and no facilities.

The 1976 women's crew at Yale was regarded as the most competitive of all the female teams. The eight were Anne Warner, Chris Ernst, Lynn Baker, Lynn Alvarez, Elaine Mathies, Cathy Pew, Chris Stowe and Jennie Kiesling. They trained hard and won meets, while the men's crew did not. In 1975, two Yale women, Chris Ernst and Anne Warner, as part of the "Red Rose Crew," won the silver-medal eight at the 1975 World Championships. Yet when the women trained at the Yale gym, the men would come and watch and jeer, calling them "sweathogs" and worse. Anne Warner remembered, "We were part of a team of men and women who didn't act like a team."

Chris Ernst had never accepted that as a woman she should be satisfied with second place in anything just because she was a woman. In high school, she joined the gymnastics team. The gym was reserved for the men's team, who refused to leave so the women could practice. Chris would challenge a male teammate: "I'll arm wrestle you, and if I win, we get to practice." She always won. She was accepted at Mount Holyoke, Smith and Yale and decided on Yale, noting, "I'll go to Yale, and I'll show them." Her mother described her as "tough, intense, very special; she always stood up for what she believed."

The Yale rowing teams had a hierarchy, dominated by the varsity heavyweights. They rowed first, they showered first and, when they had boarded the bus for the ride back to campus, the bus left, regardless of who wasn't on it. Once the ice had thawed on the river, the women endured the same frigid conditions as their male counterparts, with one major exception. Everything was controlled by the men's schedule. After the men rowed, they showered, dressed and boarded the bus. There were no showers or lockers for the women, so they just boarded the unheated bus and waited for the men to finish showering and board. They had worked as hard, trained as hard, yet, as Warner stated, "were athletes without dignity. We were soaked inside from the sweat of the practice, outside from the elements; our hair froze from the water…I caught pneumonia." They wanted the university to take them seriously, to stop talking and making excuses about the lack of showers, lockers, everything.

On March 3, 1976, they decided to do something about their treatment. In their basement locker room in the Paine Whitney Gym, they wrote "Title IX" on their bodies, front and back; put on their sweats; and proceeded to the office of Joni Barnett, the director of women's athletics. "It was very somber, quiet, tense…we knew what we were doing—a really serious moment," Warner recalled. They had arranged for a photographer and a stringer from the *New York Times* to record the event. The reporter,

David Zweig, sat in a chair, his back to the women. Nina Haight, the photographer, stood atop a desk behind the women. The women took off their sweats, exposing their naked bodies. Ernst then read the prepared statement, a "Declaration of Accountability":

> *These are the bodies Yale is exploiting. We have come here today to make clear how unprotected we are, to show graphically what we are being exposed to. On a day like today, the rain freezes on our skin. Then we sit on a bus for half an hour as the ice melts into our sweats to meet the sweat that has soaked our clothes underneath....No effective action has been taken and no matter what we hear, it doesn't make these bodies warmer, or dryer, or less prone to sickness...We are not just healthy young things in blue and white uniforms who perform feats of strength for Yale in the spring weather; we are just statistics on your win column. We're human beings and being treated as less then such.*

Zweig recalled the moment: "There was shock, surprise, hurt, pain, anger—there isn't a single word that captures what went on in those five minutes." The women then redressed and left the office.

The next day, the *New York Times* ran the story on the front page of the second section, under the headline "Yale Women Strip to Protest a Lack of Crew's Showers" with a quote from Warner: "We'll probably get showers when Peter Pan comes back to life." The press descended on the campus. Some Yalies were openly critical of the women and their protest. One remarked of the women, "They don't know who they are messing with!" That only energized the movement for change and brought results. A trailer with showers was suddenly hooked up. A year later, a full locker room for the women had been added to the boathouse. Alumni became concerned for the women's physical safety and were embarrassed. Their embarrassment changed "we can't" to "we can."

What the women, led by Christ Ernst, did changed women's athletics across the country. It had a profound ripple effect. As Cozza later said, "Had it not happened, we would not have come along as fast as we did."

After graduating from Yale with a BA in English, Chris was a coach at Yale. "In 1980, I decided to stop coaching and knew that the unions would have the big jobs under government contracts, and there would be required quotas for women and minorities, so I decided to become a plumber." In 1981, she was the first female union plumber in New Haven. In the late 1980s, she moved to Boston and today has her own firm, Pipelines, Inc.,

Chris Ernst in her plumbing office at Pipelines, Inc., outside Boston. This is a portrait of the quiet leadership that, along with her team, forever changed the treatment of female athletes when the laws and legislation couldn't.

at 1408 Centre Street, Roslindale, MA 02131 (617-327-0014), chris@ pipelinesinc.net. If one is in the Greater Boston area and needs a plumber, call Pipelines.

Changing a nation's attitude toward and treatment of others is often the result of a single, focused action. When one talks to Chris about that afternoon at Yale, she deflects any personal compliments and talks about the team. "It was a team effort," she says. "It felt like a mission—it was definitely a mission; a team mission." It may have been a team mission, but every mission needs a leader. Chris Ernst was that leader. Title IX opened the door to equality for women, but it was Chris Ernst who forced the "establishment" to respect female athletes and provide them with the same opportunities, coaches, trainers, equipment and facilities that it provided for the male athletes.

BLEEDING GREEN

Girl Scouts of Connecticut Museum

On March 21, 1912, Mrs. Juliet Low organized the first Girl Scout troop in Atlanta, Georgia. There were eighteen girls in the troop, and the merit badges were earned in two areas: homemaking and nature. Homemaking had lessons in cooking, being a hostess and doing the laundry. Nature required knowledge of trees, birds and stars, so as one leader stated, "One would develop an appreciation for the beauty of the natural scenery." In Connecticut, many troops were organized throughout the state. Some were small, others larger. As the troops grew and began to adopt the programs of the national Girl Scouts organization, there was the understandable need to re-form the individual units into a more consistent and regular organization. Such a task required a person who embraced scouting and had the leadership, vision, strength and organizational skills to bring it about. Such a person was Alice Pattison Merritt. On April 20, 1921, she was elected the commissioner of the Girl Scouts of Hartford. At the meeting, the "act of dissolving the old scout organization and incorporating the council of the Girl Scouts of Hartford county and vicinity was taken up. Action on the necessary changes in the by-laws will be made at a meeting to be held next Wednesday." The changes were made. It marked the beginning of the "modern" Girl Scouts in our state.

Alice Merritt was a formidable leader. Her husband, Joseph Merritt, was the president-treasurer of the Hartford Special Machinery Company. From 1925 to 1929, she served in the state Senate, the first woman to be elected and to serve in that chamber. During World War I, she was a Red Cross

Motor Corps officer and later was active in women's defense activities in World War II. But above it all, her great love was the Girl Scouts.

Mrs. Merritt once told a reporter that "she came into Scouting 'on the tail of my daughter's kite' when her daughter joined one of the troops in the city. She said, jokingly, that she would like to be reincarnated as a Brownie to go up through the ranks 'just to make up for what I missed as a girl.'"

Mrs. Merritt died on October 17, 1950. The *Hartford Courant* published a special editorial in tribute to her:

> *There are some who appear to have been touched by a magic wand before entering this planet. These special people go through life seemingly unaware of the qualities that make then a little more gracious, a little more understanding, a little kindlier, and a great deal more effective than the rest of us in their dealings with other people…a selfless service to her community.*

When one enters the Girl Scout Museum of Connecticut at 20 Washington Street in North Haven, straight ahead in a prominent case is the image of Mrs. Merritt, just as it should be. No other individual, short of Mrs. Low, deserves the singular honor. The museum is the result of the tireless effort of Cheryl McGuff, who, along with her husband, Steve, provided much of the hard work organizing, sorting, planning the exhibits and even helping to underwrite the initial expenses. Additional and crucial gifts came from Phyllis Palm and Peg Standley. On March 10, 2013, the ribbon was cut officially opening the Girl Scouts of Connecticut Museum.

In the Girl Scouts of Connecticut Museum, Alice Merritt is properly showcased as a focal point. To the right of the case is a "cut-out" of Mrs. Low, who founded the Girl Scouts in 1912.

The museum displays uniforms of Connecticut Girl Scouts from the early days to the present.

The museum space is small in size, but it is wonderfully packed with items, uniforms, badges, commemorative stamps, cookware, scrapbooks, handbooks and photographs, everything that celebrates the world of Girl Scouts in Connecticut. The careful and delightful orchestration of the exhibits subtly draws the visitor in, so one is looking at each and every treasured memory to be sure not to miss anything. My favorite was a small plastic Brownie bank, a rainy day fund when it is raining cats and dogs. The front of the bank has a Brownie with an umbrella and literally cats and dogs descending with the rain!

The Girl Scouts of Connecticut are still looking to collect, to preserve the record of girl scouting in our state, and welcome any donations of items or financial contributions that will let the museum grow and expand. To make a donation or to visit the museum, one should contact the CEO's office of Girls Scouts of Connecticut: 340 Washington Street, Hartford, CT 06106 (860-522-0163); www.gsofct.org. The Girl Scouts of Connecticut build girls of courage, confidence and character. The museum preserves that rich record of achievement and opens the way for today's girls to learn of the past and chart their own futures.

VANILLA BEAN CAFÉ, POMFRET

In 1988, Eileen Jessurun was taking a walk. She had turned eighteen and wondered what she was going to do with her life. She passed an old cow and carriage barn that had been built in 1848 on the corner of Routes 44, 169 and 97 in Pomfret. According to the *Sunday Telegram* newspaper, "Suddenly a logo appeared on her mental screen. It said Vanilla Bean. When I got home, I said, 'Mom, Dad, let's start a restaurant in the barn.'" With the help of brothers Barry, twenty-nine, and Brian, thirty-two, and others, they arranged to secure the barn, clean and paint the inside and install a kitchen, some seating and some posters. The initial funding came from Albert and Patricia Jessurun, and a matching loan came from Eileen's brothers. There are memories of friends pitching in, stuccoing the ceiling on a Sunday at two o'clock in the morning and hanging code-compliant sheet rock in the kitchen. On August 26, 1989, they hung up the sign, with the logo Eileen had dreamed about. The Vanilla Bean Café was open for business!

Eileen, Barry and Brian were at first the only employees, sometimes supplemented by family and friends. It started as a sixteen-seat sandwich and ice cream shop. The only seating was in the front tiled room. As Barry remembered on the eve of the opening, "We thought, 'What if nobody comes?' That ended up being the least of our worries." Soon, the lines were out the door, and they knew they had to expand. They added an outdoor patio with a grill, which more than doubled the fair-weather seating. They expanded into the barn's main space. With the increased space accommodating more and more customers, they needed to expand

The Vanilla Bean Café in Pomfret at the junction of Routes 44, 169 and 97.

the kitchen's cooking and prep areas to serve them. Within six years, they added, expanded and modified—always with the focus on serving the customer. Their philosophy has always been "create a place where we would feel comfortable and serve food that we would enjoy eating—if we wouldn't eat it, we certainly wouldn't serve it."

Because of the quality of the food and their almost obsessive attention to meeting the needs and wants of the customer, the Vanilla Bean Café, or VBC, has continued to grow. Stardom hit the place on May 8, 2002, when

Coca-Cola hosted the launch of the world premier of its new product, Vanilla Coke, at the VBC. No one has said how the corporation decided on VBC as the place to hold the event. One suspects that Barry learned of the forthcoming product and pitched it successfully. After they were chosen for the launch, he recalled, "We spent the whole month prior cleaning, painting and redoing inside and out."

I visited the VBC on a Monday in January. It was a nothing-special day, and no one knew I was coming or what I was about. The outside has ample parking. The inside is a delight. In the entrance area, the roof support timbers have been exposed, and a "penny-farthing" bicycle is stationed on one of

This is where one orders at the Vanilla Bean Café. The selection is endless and wonderful.

them. Ahead is the endless selection of offerings, with some pastry choices in the cases. There are salads, sandwiches, items from the grill, a kid's menu, a dinner menu, soups, chili, specials, quiche, desserts, a breakfast menu and, additionally, a weekend-only breakfast menu. Everything is prepared on-site. In the main seating area of the barn, the walls are painted a warm color; they are used as an art gallery for works by local artists that are for sale. One hundred percent of the sale price goes to the artist; VBC does not take a commission. After one places an order, he is handed an oversized playing card. This way, when the order is ready, it is brought to the customer identified by the number on the card, whether to eat there or take out. There is no one shattering the atmosphere shouting, "Number seven, your order is ready!" Throughout the year, VBC, usually on Saturday nights, hosts various folk groups, groups from the Pomfret School and evenings to benefit the local food bank, and the café is on the National Music Circuit. Its website www.TheVanillaBeanCafe.com can provide one with performance schedules and updates.

While I was there, I could not help but notice the steady stream of customers. Some stayed and ate, others did takeout. Some seemed to have been there before; others, like me, were first-timers. I look forward to going back.

LEROY ANDERSON'S HOUSE

A year ago, I attended a meeting of the State Historic Preservation Review Board as a spectator. The first item on the agenda for nomination to the National Register of Historic Places was, to my surprise, the Leroy Anderson House. Was this *the* Leroy Anderson who composed "Sleigh Ride" and "Blue Tango"? My mind began to race through various titles—"The Typewriter" and "Plink, Plank, Plunk!" (the theme for television's *I've Got a Secret*). I didn't know he lived in Connecticut. I associated him with Arthur Fiedler and the Boston Pops and assumed he lived in Massachusetts.

Leroy Anderson was born in Boston on June 29, 1908. His parents were Swedish and had come to America as children. Both his parents were musical; his mother was a church organist and pianist and his father a postal employee who played the mandolin. Anderson learned to play the piano and organ sitting on his mother's lap. At age eleven, he composed a minuet for string quartet, which was shown to George Chadwick, the dean of the New England Conservatory. Chadwick awarded Anderson a scholarship to study at the conservatory. He took up the double bass and studied organ, and his father encouraged him to learn the trombone so he could march with the Harvard University Band at football games. In 1925, he entered Harvard College as a music major. According to Steve Metcalf, in *Leroy Anderson: A Bio-Bibliography*, "His most influential Teacher was the American composer Walter Piston, who joined the faculty in 1926…His flinty, solidly built music was receiving a growing number of performances, eventually including many by the Boston Symphony Orchestra." Among Piston's other students were Elliott Carter, Gail Kubik and Leonard Bernstein. Anderson credited Piston with teaching the composer to be objective: "The general tendency of a composer is to fall in love with what he does. Piston advised us to listen to our compositions as though someone else had written them."

Because of his father's advice, he did win a place in the Harvard band, playing the trombone. In his senior year, he became the director of the band. He graduated in 1929, magna cum laude, and was elected to Phi Beta Kappa. The next year, he received his MA. He applied for the Paine Traveling Fellowship but was turned down, in part because the chair of the Music Department did not approve of the Harvard Band as a worthy group. Anderson resigned from the band as director, reapplied and was again rejected, so he resumed his role as the band's director. He studied for a PhD in languages and made ends meet by tutoring in music, serving as choral director and organist at a local church, playing in various orchestras and serving as a freelance arranger.

In Moore's book on Arthur Fiedler, Anderson recalled that George Judd, manager of the Boston Pops, asked him to arrange some Harvard songs for the Pops Harvard Night. "So I wrote this piece, which I called 'Harvard Fantasy'…and then at the appropriate point during the concert Fiedler called me out, and I conducted this and a few other college songs. It was quite a thrill." When the concert was over, Fiedler "said to me, 'Anderson! You orchestrate well! How about doing something for us?'" It marked a turning point. It was the start of a remarkable relationship between Anderson, the Pops and Fiedler. Two years later, Anderson composed "Jazz Pizzicato" and later, at Fiedler's request, a companion piece, "Jazz Legato," so he could record both on one side of a 78rpm disc.

In 1942, he was drafted and went to Iceland as a translator and interpreter for U.S. counterintelligence. Later, he was reassigned to Military Intelligence Service in Washington. Fiedler stayed in touch and asked Anderson to write something for the Pops' Army Night. Anderson composed "Promenade" and then, as he was scoring the work, another composition came to mind. "It occurred to me that hundreds of composers had written music imitating or suggesting clocks but that all these clocks were ordinary ones that beat a regular rhythm. No one had described a 'syncopated' clock," certainly not one that lost its mainspring at the end. On May 28, 1945, with a three-day pass, he premiered both for the Pops in uniform.

After the war, Anderson continued to compose, and in 1950 he began recording his "orchestral miniatures." WCBS-TV heard his recording of "The Syncopated Clock" and decided to use it as the theme for its program of old movies, *The Late Show.* His 1951 "Blue Tango" sold over one million records, was twenty-two weeks on the Hit Parade and won him a gold record and a slot on jukeboxes across America. Anderson appeared on *The Ed Sullivan Show.* In 1953, a study by the American Symphony Orchestra League had Anderson as the composer whose works were most frequently performed by American orchestras, ahead of Copland, Gershwin and Barber.

After he was drafted on October 31, 1942, Anderson married Eleanor Firke, from Illinois, whom he met at the International House in New York, where Anderson played the piano. They would have four children: Jane, Eric, Rolf and Kurt. With the success of his pieces, they moved to Woodbury and in 1953 hired Joseph Stein to design a house for them. Stein had studied under Walter Gropius at Harvard. The house is a low-slung Modernist residence on the south side of a country road, on a nearly twelve-acre site. On a classic fall day, I was invited to visit the home by Rolf and Anderson's widow. The house sits atop a knoll and has a flat roof with an overall horizontal profile. It is finished with red-painted cedar siding and windows that look out over the wooded countryside.

The Leroy Anderson House was designed by Joseph Stein in 1953 for the composer and his family. Note the swing on the tree.

Inside, the house looks as if it had not changed since the family moved in. Each room has a special story about the composer and his family. With Rolf as my guide, we began in the library:

> *This is where Dad would work in the morning, doing his business correspondence. His books are all in place. We always knew what time of day it was by where Dad was in the house—mornings in the library; then lunch; orchestrations in the afternoon in the "workroom" [which is soundproofed]; four to five, recreational reading; then supper. After supper, he would go for slow walks, for an hour or two, composing in his head, working out a theme or a composition.*

The house, immaculately cared for, is still his home, where time stopped in the mid-1950s. The workroom with the spinet piano, the living room with the Steinway baby grand, the dining room area, even the wood swing on rope cords on the nearby tree, are of Anderson and his family.

Perhaps his most popular piece is "Sleigh Ride," which, according to Rolf, he thought of during a blistering heat wave in the summer of 1946 while digging trenches in Woodbury. He was trying to locate the pipes that once brought spring water to his mother-in-law's house. Mrs. Anderson remembered him coming into the house, shirtless and dripping from the heat, and jotting a few notes. Steve Metcalf describes the piece as his "most sophisticated miniature... we can safely say that no other work of music can claim the following specific roster of interpreters: The New York Philharmonic, the Ronettes, Alvin and the Chipmonks, Johnny Mathis, the Canadian Brass, the Ventures, Ella Fitzgerald, Captain Kangaroo, and the Mormon Tabernacle Choir." It should be noted that when Fiedler first performed it in 1948, it was an orchestral piece without lyrics. Jack Mills, Anderson's publisher, initiated the idea of having Mitchell Parish write the lyrics. Like most composers, according to Rolf, Anderson was concerned that the lyrics might totally revise the work, "but he was willing to listen." Mrs. Anderson recalled, "Mitchell did his work by himself and showed it to Leroy when it was done. I think it is true to say Leroy was surprised at how much he liked the results." The lyrics with the music have made "Sleigh Ride" a holiday classic.

There are many Anderson stories and reminiscences, but two, reported by Richard Stevenson in the *Litchfield County Times*, are worth sharing here: "Leroy Anderson was a man who liked to do his own work around the family house in Woodbury, and on an autumn day long ago he was raking leaves in his front yard when a carload of celebrity seekers pulled up and one of them

Leroy Anderson with the sheet music covers of two of his best-known works: "The Syncopated Clock" and "Sleigh Ride." *Leroy Anderson Foundation.*

asked, 'Is this where Leroy Anderson lives?' 'Yes it is,' replied the composer-conductor, 'but he's not home just now.'"

The other was shared by Gregg Herr, who was in a scout troop that met at the house. At some point in the meeting, he slipped away, went upstairs

Just as Gregg Herr remembered: "There in a bright room with a glass wall was a gleaming black grand piano." Anderson would work out his compositions here and in the "workroom." *Leroy Anderson Foundation.*

and peeked into the living room. "There in a bright room with a glass wall was a gleaming black grand piano. Seated at the piano was Leroy Anderson, deeply engrossed in his work. He would play a few phrases, write something down with a pencil and then play some more. I was absolutely spellbound with what I saw and heard, for I realized that he was creating something entirely new. I was listening to his music at the exact moment of its creation, and no one else in the world could ever have that unique experience—no one!"

The Leroy Anderson Foundation has been most thoughtful about caring for the legacy of Anderson. It donated his scores and personal papers to the Gilmore Music Library at Yale University. The Harvard Theatre Collection has also established an archive relating to Anderson, the Boston Pops and "Harvardiana." The foundation has a website, and periodically the house is open to the public.

RUDY ZALLINGER AND THE PEABODY MUSEUM'S *THE AGE OF REPTILES*

Rudolph "Rudy" Zallinger was born in 1919 in Irkutsk, Siberia, to Franz, an Austrian POW during World War I, and Maria, who was Polish but working in Russia. They had met in a factory where Franz was hand-painting china and Maria was in sales. When Lenin ordered the release of all war prisoners, they traveled with Rudy toward Manchuria. In Harbin, Rudy had caught the measles; they left the train, and he was hospitalized. While Rudy recovered, Franz made a living painting signs and murals, saving what funds he could for them to immigrate to America. In 1923, Franz left first and settled in Seattle, Washington. The next year, Maria came with Rudy and his sister, Wanda. According to Rudy's daughter Lisa David, "Franz became a naturalized citizen in the shortest possible time prescribed by law, and he insisted that when his family arrived, they would live in an American neighborhood, not in a colony of immigrants…Paint was always around the house, and Rudy started early; he would clean his father's paint brushes before he could brush his own teeth." He attended his first life painting class in 1929, when he was ten. In 1937, he received a scholarship for a painting tutorial on the East Coast. The teacher persuaded Rudy not to attend the University of Washington, where he had been accepted into its arts program, but to attend Yale University's fine arts program. He was in the class of 1942.

George Peabody was born on February 18, 1795, in South Danvers, Massachusetts. The town later changed its name in his honor. Apprenticed to a dry goods merchant at eleven, at age fifteen he began to make his fortune. At twenty, he was a partner in a wholesale dry goods business and within seven years was worth a reported $40,000, a considerable sum at the time. In 1837, he established the George Peabody Company banking house in London. He underwrote the education of his nephew Othniel Charles Marsh at Yale. In 1866, at Marsh's urging, Peabody established the Peabody Museum of Natural History, and Marsh was appointed the professor of paleontology. When Peabody died in 1869, he was honored by burial in Westminster Abbey and then was buried as he wished in Peabody, Massachusetts.

In his senior year, Rudy took a job illustrating seaweed for Albert Parr, the Peabody's director. The museum was drab and boring. It had a great collection of dinosaur skeleton bones—stegosaurus, edmontosaurus, Apatosaurus—but the walls were gray, the floor was gray, the bones were gray and the room was gray. As Rudy recalled, "Parr had this wall in the museum and a lot of gray bones. He thought it ought to be spruced up. Lewis York, head of the art school, suggested that I paint it." Instead of a series of isolated panels, Rudy suggested a giant panorama, a 110-foot-long, 16-foot-high mural: *The Age of Reptiles*. It would take five years to complete, from 1942 to 1947.

As Rudy stated, "The curriculum at the Yale School of the Fine Arts did not include a course in the painting of dinosaurs, so I undertook an eighteen-month crash course on the animals and plants that would be portrayed." His teachers were Yale's legendary Richard Swann Lull, nearly eighty; G. Edward Lewis; George Wieland; and Harvard's Alfred Romer. The next step was to prepare the creation of the working drawing where various compositions would be tried, revised, redrawn or eliminated until the final scheme had been accepted.

As the main entrance to the hall is near the right side of the mural, and as that is also the chronological progression of the fossils, the mural needed to be drawn from right to left and not the traditional left to right. In October 1943, the wall had been prepared and plastered, and Rudy had completed the full-color egg tempera panel. He then began working on the actual wall. He divided the wall into two-foot squares that corresponded to the squares on the panel. With charcoal in hand, he began drawing on the wall. After the line drawing was completed, he began the detailed monochrome underpainting. The forms "were deliberately overmodeled so that traces would later show through the overpainted layering of colors. These first paint films were restricted to a medium tonality for the light sides of forms and a matrix coating for the darker parts."

Rudy Zallinger, working with a sketch on his lap, painting the underpainting for *Edaphosaurus* in 1944. Because of his meticulous underpainting, and later careful "floating" of washes of colors, the mural has a mystical quality of light. *Courtesy Peabody Museum of Natural History, Yale University, New Haven, Connecticut.*

Zallinger's depiction of the apatosaurus (brontosaurus) in the mural that has been featured on magazine covers, postage stamps and billboards—sometimes facing left, sometimes right—but an iconic image, always recognizable. It should face to the right. The Age of Reptiles, *a mural by Rudolph F. Zallinger, Copyright 1966, 1985, 1989, Peabody Museum of Natural History, Yale University, New Haven, Connecticut.*

One is struck by the vibrant luminosity and clarity of detail that the mural presents, even at a distance. As Rudy explained, "The later phases, most time-consuming because of their complexities, involved the elaboration of modulation of tones, lines and shapes in order to achieve the intended illusions—the final three-dimensional appearance of the work. The technique, called *fresco secco* [from the Italian *fresco*, plaster, and *secco*, dry]." It allows the artist to "feature the pure essences of pigment individualities." This is the meticulous underpainting; the floating of layers of color to create the desired gradual shading, luminosity and depth gives the mural, its landscape, animals and foliage, a sense of vibrancy, movement and action with incredible detail. The mural was completed in June 1947. In 1949, Rudy received a Pulitzer Fellowship in Art in recognition of this achievement. Rudy went to Seattle to work as a freelance artist.

Richard C. Lee, later mayor of New Haven, was the head of Yale's News Bureau. He brought to the attention of the editors of *Life* magazine Rudy's mural and suggested they should consider it for their forthcoming "The World We Live In" series. On September 7, 1953, Rudy's mural was on the cover of *Life*, although they flipped it to meet their graphic designs. In 1970, the mural was featured on a U.S. postage stamp, "The Age of Reptiles," and was correctly positioned.

Rudy returned to Yale as a Fellow in Geology. *Life* commissioned him to paint *The Age of Mammals*, which was published in 1953 but not executed as a mural at the museum until 1967. He was a professor at the University of Hartford's Art School. In 1986, he was commissioned by Aetna Life and Casualty to paint the mural *Early History of Hartford* for its offices on Capital Avenue. It was his last mural. It is today at the Hartford Public Library's main branch in "The American Place" section. Rudolph Zallinger died on August 1, 1995, at the age of seventy-five.

FOUNTAIN HILL CEMETERY

Fountain Hill Cemetery is forty-eight acres of rolling hills in Deep River, Connecticut. Founded in 1851, it is a classic example of the "rural cemetery" so popular in the late nineteenth century. One enters the cemetery off High Street through a set of ornamental gates, designed in the Gothic Revival style, a gift from Reverend Russell Jennings. He owned and operated the Jennings Manufacturing Company. The road winds casually around the trees and outcropping of rock, recalling an early visitor's description:

> *The special attractiveness of Fountain Hill Cemetery consists not in its monuments, but in itself, in its own natural beauty as heightened by art. Its park-like spaces, shaded with a variety of deciduous and evergreen trees; its umbrageous ravines; its soft and graceful slopes, broken here and there with picturesque masses of rock, and the frequent glimpses of diversified scenery that everywhere gratify the eye, unite in making a scene of summer or autumnal beauty that is rarely found in association with the dead, and cannot fail to have an elevating and refining influence upon the living.*

The layout of the cemetery is in keeping with the rural movement, and its ridges are appropriately named Twilight Ridge, Spruce Hill, Mount Hope, Crescent Hill and Sunset Ridge, to name a few. The cemetery presents the story of the community. The earliest stones are plain and rectangular, rough-cut fieldstone with descriptive epitaphs; a young child's marker has "Blighted Hope"; a veteran's, "A Christian Patriot Sleeps." Captain Palmer's stone records that he was murdered by "the Negro cook" aboard his ship, *Eudora*, in 1855. Over six hundred veterans are buried in the cemetery. Of note is the plain granite monument of John Simonton, a black Spanish-American War veteran from North Carolina. The tallest monument is that of Captain Samuel Mather. He was a clipper ship captain who set records sailing from Connecticut to Australia. The white marble obelisk has on its central plaque his ship *Nightingale*, framed by rope carvings. He died in the Civil War in 1862. The monument was erected in 1868

Captain Mather's monument at Fountain Hill Cemetery features his ship *Nightingale*, framed by rope carvings.

and was reported to have cost over $5,000. There is also the grave of the bank robber, which is carved with the letters "XYZ." Legend records that it was often visited by a woman dressed all in black who left flowers at the marker and then quietly disappeared.

George Read, a prominent businessman, is considered the founder of Deep River. As a deacon in the Baptist Church, he started the First National Bank in his home and the church in his parlor. He was also president of the Deep River Savings Bank and was a prime mover of the Fountain Hill Cemetery Association. He brought the landscape architect B.F. Hathaway from Stamford, Connecticut, to lay out the roads and the landscaping. Following Hathaway's plan, the cemetery has carefully delineated boundaries, separating the peace within from the busy world without. The chapel near the entrance was given by Mary Wooster, granddaughter of George Read. Designed by Isaac Allen of Hartford, its site was blasted to allow the building to appear to emerge from the granite ridge.

The grave markers in Fountain Hill document the evolution of Deep River from a village of some 200 to a town of over 1,200. They chronicle

America and its growth from rural ambiance to an industrial center. Here one visually reads the names of the immigrants who came and worked in the town—the Irish escaping the famine; Italians who were skilled stone cutters and worked in the quarries; Germans, Poles, Russians and Swedes, among others—all seeking the American hope for a new life.

CONSTITUTION PLAZA

If It Had Been Built as Designed

C onstitution Plaza is the name given to the twelve-acre Front-State-Market Street district, northeast of Hartford's Old State House. Traditionally, it was a marginal area, where immigrants lived upon arriving in the city and where workers at Hartford's eighteen docks lived—an area that flooded in the spring and the fall. It was a slum. Once one had accumulated a few resources, the first thing one did was leave, move out, to higher ground. Today, there is great nostalgia for this lower east side. As former mayor the late James Kinsella noted, "Nostalgia diminishes the scent of rotting structures, the sight of rat infestation and the grief caused by disease and poor health." This area was less than two blocks from Hartford's business district and only a block from its shopping district. The twelve acres were sparsely occupied by 108 "marginal" businesses and 187 families and 31 individuals living in tenements.

Hartford established a Redevelopment Agency in March 1950, and its first task was to see if this area qualified for federal Title I funding, which provided subsidies to pay for replacing congested downtown districts with urban renewal. In 1952, Hartford was granted Title I assistance with which to plan what should replace the slum. Legal questions stalled the project until 1954. In 1956, voters, by a four-to-one margin, approved the $800,000 bond issue to cover the local one-third of the project's cost. In June 1958, after all the remaining business and individuals had relocated, the mayor threw a brick through an abandoned building's window, signaling the start of the demolition.

Four developers presented plans for the site. Cliff Strike of F.H. McGraw and Company was the winning developer. In concert with the Connecticut Natural Gas Corporation and architect Charles DuBose, the concept was an all-inclusive visionary plan for the future of the city. The buildings would be heated and cooled by centralized underground systems provided by the gas company, eliminating the need for separate heating and cooling plants in each of the structures. Conceived as an extension of the retail-shopping district just one block to the west, the height of the plaza was the same elevation as the Brown-Thomson Department Store at Main Street, seventy and a half feet above sea level. There would be a land bridge down Temple Street connecting Main Street to the Plaza, centered on the clock tower. Beneath the land bridge, DuBose associate Jack Dollard designed a festive open-air market. The plaza was on a platform above the parking garage for 3,500 cars. To the east of the plaza, it was planned to build the new civic center and sports coliseum and convention center. To the north, it was planned to have housing units—a village—joining the plaza with the Hartford Graduate Center. On the north was the new office complex anchored by the chamber of commerce. There was consideration of having a Playboy Club there, but that was thought to be too risky for this Yankee city. The City Club took its place. Flanking the chamber's building, on the west and east, were two one-story wings for retail. On the east, these would include Brentano's Bookstore and W.J. Sloane home furnishings. On the west side were Rogers Peet men's clothier, Layne Brant women's fashions, Bridal Party Penthouse and more. In the center was a giant scaled bonsai garden, Willow Court. Six oval mounds of green grass with sculptured willow trees, bordered by bands of white granite, were suspended above the pool of black hexagonal tiles. As the water gently flowed from beneath the mounds, it covered the black tiles, creating a glistening and refreshing effect before tumbling into the pebbled troughs. Sasaki Walker and Associates designed this and a series of complimentary water gardens on the plaza, carefully created to refresh the visitor and provide a sound barrier from the noise of the street. The Connecticut Bank and Trust building at One Constitution Plaza and the Hartford National Bank building at 100 were designed with their top floors as apartments for people to live in the heart of the city. The Hotel Americana was built on the east side for visitors. A second hotel was erected just to the north. A restaurant building was placed centrally south of Willow Court to provide an oasis for visitors. The plaza extended to the south with a land bridge over State Street connecting

Constitution Plaza as it looked soon after it was completed.

to the Phoenix Building, the world's first two-sided building. Nicknamed "the boat building," it was designed by Harrison & Abramovitz.

Great care had been given to connect the new plaza with the rest of the city. The land bridge down Temple Street extended the existing shopping district to the shops at the same level on the plaza. Mrs. Auerbach of G. Fox and Co. Department Store added a wing and entrance on the store's Market Street side to embrace the plaza and draw its customers into her store. Hartford National Bank's 100 Constitution Plaza Building had a monumental façade by sculptor Isamu Noguchi on the Market Street side to draw attention to it at the street level. Stores such as Rogers Peet had entrances on Market Street and on the plaza. The CBS television station affiliate WTIC, today WFSB, then a property of Travelers Insurance Corporation, agreed to build its new facility, Broadcast House, on the southeast corner of the plaza. They appeared to have thought of everything—parking for cars, connected to the existing shopping district, a hotel, more shops, restaurants, commercial entities, convenient to the planned coliseum and convention center, housing, et cetera—so why didn't DuBose's vision achieve its potential? Why didn't it work to revitalize the city?

The 1960s were marked by a strained economy. The Travelers Corporation, which had provided F.H. McGraw with the overall financing for the project, ended up owning the project. Because of the economy, major steps were taken to reduce the project. The land bridge between the plaza and the existing shopping district on Main Street was eliminated, leaving the plaza aloof, unconnected and alone. Politicians moved the coliseum and convention center from east of the plaza to the west in the city, on Trumbull Street. Conservative actuarial bean counters at Travelers revised the plans. Gone were the apartments in the towers. Those tenants would require services twenty-four/seven; businesses needed services only eight hours, five days a week. As for the restaurant building on the plaza, the city couldn't figure out how to let it have a liquor permit as the sidewalk around it was private property. Such permits for public restaurants went only to establishments with public sidewalks. It became a brokerage house. One by one, Strike and DuBose's vision was diluted and eviscerated. The concept of connecting people with services with stores with businesses with housing with education centers was revised or eliminated with disastrous results.

Several years ago, I had the privilege of showing Alexander Gavin, author of *The American City: What Works, What Doesn't*, Constitution Plaza. He had been more than critical of the project. As we walked the area, I explained Strike and Dubose's vision: the connecting land bridge to Main Street, centrally focused on the clock tower; the projected coliseum and civic center; the housing; the business centers as additional anchors; the apartments in the office towers; the hotels and spaces for restaurants and stores; the additional housing and educational center. He could see that this was not planned as an isolated elevated platform but as an extension of the existing spaces, amenities, businesses and housing. Midway through the tour, he turned, paused and said, "If they had built it as planned, it would have worked."

If one walks the plaza today, do not judge it by what remains. The existing shards bear no resemblance to the thoughtful and visionary planning and the exquisite creative design that conceived it. If it had been built as planned, all of it, the center of Hartford would be thriving, and the suburban malls might never have been built as there would not have been a reason for their existence.

GOODSPEED OPERA HOUSE

Where Annie, Man of La Mancha *and* Others Were Born

Today, the name Vivien Kellems is not a household name. In the 1950s and '60s, she was the multimillionaire industrialist, founder of the Connecticut Cable Grip Company and more than a force to be reckoned with. Her cable invention supported bridges around the world, including the George Washington Bridge. As a maiden lady, she strongly objected to the tax codes and fiercely lobbied the U.S. Congress about providing tax equity for single taxpayers. As a maverick Republican, she ran for governor in 1954. As a resident of East Haddam, she spearheaded the group that saved the Goodspeed Opera House from demolition. Herman Wolf wrote on the thirtieth anniversary of Goodspeed, "It was she who saved the opera house." She did not do it alone, and she would not have claimed that she did. She was well aware that her strong convictions and deep resources, and the fact that many would acknowledge that at times it was easier to give her what she wanted than to fight her, could indeed turn the tide of the causes she advocated. Her place in the preservation of the Goodspeed is often overlooked, but without her presence and resources, it is doubtful that the structure would have been saved.

In 1958, local residents, including Libby Kaye and Mrs. Alfred Terry, and others, including Kellems, began the effort to save the Goodspeed from demolition. The six-story building, built by William H. Goodspeed, was a theater not an opera house. It was in fact a multipurpose building: general store, post office and dentist's office with a theater on the upper two stories. It had for years been a storage facility for the Connecticut Department of

Transportation. All the seating had been removed, and it was a tough road to imagine how it might be restored and if it could meet existing fire and life safety codes, let alone be a successful and sustainable theater. It was off the beaten track in the town of East Haddam, where many of the residents were, and apparently still are, not sure that having a theater was good for the town. The Goodspeed could have a maximum seating of only 398. The stage is tiny by theatrical standards: twenty feet from front to back and forty-three feet from side wall to side wall, and the proscenium opening is a mere twenty-seven feet by fifteen feet. Fredrick Palmer of the architectural firm of Schutz and Goodwin designed the "re-creation" of the interior space, creating the grand stair; restored the main seating and balcony areas; and provided for the elevators and interior stairs to meet the codes. Palmer's designs provided the Goodspeed with the look that creates a fantasy so that when one entered the front doors, with the great faux marble stair, he knew he was indeed in a special place, for a special performance. It was no small effort. Leo Sans and Company, who would later work on the restoration of the Twain House, was hired to restore the interior decorations of the main theater. On June 19, 1963, the curtain went up on the "new" Goodspeed Opera House with the show *Oh, Lady! Lady!* by Kern, Bolton and Wodehouse. Governor Dempsey, Beatrice Rosenthal and Kellems were there for the grand reopening of the iconic building on the Connecticut River.

Michael Price, a student at the Yale School of Drama, helped open the first season under Albert Selden. "Back then," he recalled, "Goodspeed was presenting shows in the summer stock tradition—one week this, one week that. I was young and knew better. I had all the answers. I was not invited back." After a series of directors and management changes, Price was brought back, first to the management side and then placed in charge as executive director in 1969. He produced *Peter Pan*, and it was a hit. The 1970 season didn't fare as well, and in 1971, the financial situation was bleak until *Hubba Hubba*, the World War II stage-door canteen show, was a hit. The Goodspeed began to focus on its niche: reviving classic musicals and premiering new works. It branded itself as the "Home of the American Musical." Patrons would surprise themselves as they descended the great stair, singing "Everybody wants to know, how to do the tickle toe" or other tunes previously forgotten but revived at Goodspeed, and would be greeted at the bottom of the stairs by Michael himself. He always seemed to remember everyone's name. He has been for so many years indelibly a part of the Goodspeed experience.

On an October afternoon, Michael Price and I were in his sun-filled office in the Goodspeed. We have known each other since the 1970s, when we served on the state arts commission. The walls are upholstered with tributes, mementoes, photos, certificates and salutations. A barber chair holds court by the window. His desk is focused and organized: computer, pad, pencil, period. It was as focused as the Michael I had known. In conversation, I realized that he had begun to loosen up a little, which for him was a lot. I began to ask my questions, some about the Goodspeed, some about Michael. He paused, looked obliquely at me and asked, "Is this about me or Goodspeed?" "Both," I replied, for as he has been the driving force for over forty years, the two are inseparable. I later learned that he is being less controlling, and this has allowed the staff to grow, to become more engaged, and, in

Michael Price in front of the Goodspeed Opera House. He has been the guiding force since 1969. *Goodspeed Opera House.*

Michael's words, "it took a while for the staff to realize I really was trusting them and was trying to stop doing everything. They have blossomed and grown in so many ways. They are doing a great job."

"What was the biggest surprise musical?" I asked.

"*Annie*," he replied without pausing. The Goodspeed premiered it in 1976. "She doesn't even have red hair until the third act. The dog Sandy came from the Connecticut Humane Society, and the public loved the show. The public still loves the show." *Annie* is one of many shows that have premiered at the Goodspeed and gone on to Broadway, including *Man of La Mancha*, *Something's Afoot*, *Shenandoah*, *Very Good Eddie*, *Whoppee*, *The Five O'Clock Girl*, *Harrigan 'n' Hart*, *Take Me Along*, *Oh, Kay!*, *The Most Happy Fella*, *Gentleman Prefer Blondes*, *Swinging on a Star*, *By Jeeves*, *All Shook Up* and *The Story of My Life*. Taking a show from the Goodspeed's tiny stage to Broadway is not as easy as it seems. "It is a total redesign of the entire production—sets, chorography, often the cast, everything. Of course, we are excited at the opportunity and

The musical *Annie* had its world premier at Goodspeed in 1976. It starred Andrea McArdle in the title role, with Reid Shelton. *Goodspeed Opera House, William Brownell, photographer.*

the challenge, but one doesn't just move East Haddam to New York City without critical adaptations and changes."

The Goodspeed's fiftieth-anniversary season will have on its main stage *Good News*, *Hello Dolly* and *The Most Happy Fella*. It will also mark Price's forty-fifth year at the helm of the iconic building. Price at the Goodspeed has broken all the rules—its out-of-the-mainstream location, tiny stage and limited seating—and made it a must-go-to place. It is an intimate experience, with quality musicals; you'll leave humming the tunes. The Goodspeed experience is all that Kellems, Terry and the pioneers who saved the opera house hoped it would be. It has taken a lot of hard, hard work. When one has a ticket for a show, the attendee has a ticket for a place that gives back as no other place does. Michael Price and his team have made that a reality. Subscribe today!

LEDGE LIGHTHOUSE

A t the mouth of the Thames River and the entrance to New London
Harbor is a distinctive French Second Empire–style chateau surrounded
by water. It is a lighthouse; in fact, it is Ledge Lighthouse. It is unlike any
lighthouse one will ever see anywhere.

Connecticut's New London Harbor is at the extreme end of Long Island
Sound on the Thames River. It is a protected harbor, making it an ideal
location for whaling ships. There are, however, a number of submerged
shoals and ledges that make navigation into the harbor extremely dangerous
in foggy or rough weather. The first New London Light was built in 1761. In
the early 1900s, New London was transitioning from a whaling center to an
industrial city. The existing light wasn't strong enough to direct boats around
the ledges at the entrance to the harbor. Petitions for a new lighthouse at the
entrance began in 1890. In 1903, the Lighthouse Board recommended:

> *The necessity for establishing a light and an efficient fog signal in such a
> position as to enable vessels to enter and leave the harbor of New London,
> Conn., has become evident, and especially so for the aid of those approaching
> from seaward. The numerous outlying shoals and ledges surrounding the
> entrance to this harbor make it dangerous in thick weather…it is suggested
> that a light and fog signal station be established.*

The initial appropriation authorized by the United States Senate in 1906
was for $115,000. The actual cost is believed to have been $250,000.

Ledge Lighthouse is the iconic landmark that marks the Connecticut coastline. It is preserved by the New London Ledge Lighthouse Foundation. *Connecticut Office of Culture and Tourism; Kindra Clineff, photographer.*

The curious design of Ledge Light is believed to have been demanded by two wealthy individuals whose summer estates overlooked the entrance of the harbor: Morton Plant of New York City and Avery Point, Groton son of railroad tycoon Henry B. Plant, and Edward Stephen Harkness of New York City and Waterford, whose family had been early investors in Standard Oil. It was Harkness's mother who, following the death of her son Charles, gave $3 million to Yale to build the Harkness Memorial Quadrangle (Harkness Tower). According to legend, they understood the need for a light at the entrance to the harbor but refused to have their views compromised by a typical conical can or "sparkplug."

The actual location of Ledge Light is latitude 41 degrees, 18 minutes north; longitude 72 degrees, 5 minutes west. To aid navigation, the building's four corners mark the points of the compass. The three-story "house" is made of brick; its windowsills and corner details are granite. Atop the mansard roof and dormer windows is the cast-iron lantern. The lantern originally held a fourth-order Fresnel lens from the Henry-Lepaute Company of Paris, with an incandescent oil vapor lamp. The clockwork mechanism had to be wound every four hours to keep the lens revolving.

In 1908, the contract to build the lighthouse was awarded to the T.A. Scott Company of New London. Work began on July 10, 1908, on T.A. Scott property in Groton. A large crib fifty-two feet square and thirty-five feet high was constructed using 160,000 board feet of yellow pine and nine tons of iron and steel. On August 18, 1908, the crib was towed by three tugboats down the Thames River, eventually reaching its permanent location above the Southwest Ledge. It was filled with rock riprap and approximately 3,500 barrels of cement and sunk in 28 feet of water. An additional riprap deposit, 82 feet square and 10 feet deep, was placed around the foundation to protect it. The concrete pier, 50 feet square and 18 feet high, was built on top of the crib as the foundation for the lighthouse. The Hamilton R. Douglas Company of New London was then contracted by T.A. Scott to build the lighthouse.

The New London Ledge Light is maintained by the New London Ledge Lighthouse Foundation. The best way to visit the lighthouse is with Project Oceanology (www.oceanology.org). The tours are in July, August and September, and one must reserve ahead. I went out on the *Environ-lab II* under the command of Captain Rafferty. The twenty-some-minute trip from the Avery Point dock to Ledge Light is breathtaking. At the light, we disembarked and were greeted by Todd Gipstein, president of the new London Ledge Lighthouse Foundation, the group of dedicated volunteers who lease the

To reach Ledge Lighthouse, one should book passage with Project Oceanology in Groton (www. Oceanology.org). Once there, one is welcomed by Todd Gipstein, president of the nonprofit foundation that is preserving the building.

building from the Coast Guard and maintain, paint, repair and protect it from the elements. The foundation is a chapter of the American Lighthouse Foundation. If one is interested in volunteering or donating to help preserve this landmark, e-mail Info@LedgeLighthouse.org. Todd provided a brief history and what there was to see and do. On entering the building, it feels more like a stately home on Park Avenue than a lighthouse. The central stair climbs up two floors to the light. One is sixty-eight feet above the sea and has a totally unobstructed view! As visitors descend, they pass the former bedrooms for the keepers, a kitchen, a dining room and lounge areas. In the basement were a cistern, furnace and working equipment for the light. Inside, the foundation has created interesting and informative history panels, and volunteers guide one's visit and answer questions.

Some of those who were stationed at the light enjoyed it; others did not. Allegedly, the light is haunted by a keeper named Ernie who served there in the 1920s or 1930s. One day, he learned his wife had run off with a ferryboat captain. Left alone and distraught, he snapped, went to the roof and jumped. Ever since, keepers have claimed he haunts the lighthouse.

Ledge Light went into service on November 10, 1909. The *New London Day* reported that the light could be seen up to eighteen miles away. Characteristic: three white flashes followed by red every thirty seconds. The foghorn, added in 1911, sounds two blasts every twenty seconds. Ledge Light survived many storms and hurricanes, including the 1938 Hurricane, but could not survive as a manned light. In 1987, Ledge Light was the last lighthouse on Long Island Sound to be automated. On the last day, a coast guardsman wrote the following in the lighthouse's log: "Rock of slow torture. Ernie's domain.

Hell on earth—may New London Ledge's light shine on forever because I'm through. I will watch it from afar while drinking a brew."

What does a landmark such as Ledge Light really mean? The following is from the Ledge Light orientation film (copyright Todd A. Gipstein):

> *We were out in a terrible storm, coming up the coast of Connecticut. We were scared. The helmsman fought the wheel. We were looking for Ledge Lighthouse to guide us into New London.*
>
> *The storm battered us. And then came the cry "Ledge Light to starboard!" And we all saw it. That beacon in the darkness, telling us where we were, where to go.*
>
> *When you've been out at sea in a storm or at night, you really know what that lighthouse means. To a mariner, it says, "You are home. You are safe."*

JUST WALKING THE DOG OR CAT

The Connecticut Humane Society

In the summer before her senior year (1880) at Hartford Public High School, Gertrude O. Lewis was vacationing with her family in New Hampshire, near the White Mountains. Upon learning that George Angell, the president of the Massachusetts Society for the Prevention of Cruelty to Animals, was staying nearby, she paid him a visit. Mr. Angell recalled:

> *I was called upon at my hotel by a modest schoolgirl from Hartford, Connecticut…She told me how much she had suffered from the cruelties inflicted on animals in her State, there being no society for their protection, and she asked me if I could not do anything to stop them. I said, "When you go home, see if you can't get a meeting in some of your churches on a Saturday evening, and on my way to Washington, where I am to spend the winter, I will stop and lecture, and we will see what can be done."*

Upon her return to Hartford, Gertrude enlisted her pastor, the Reverend Joseph Twitchell of the Asylum Hill Congregational Church, to help in her cause. He wrote a letter to fellow clergymen and parishioners on October 19, 1880, introducing Gertrude: "Her cause is that of the prevention of cruelty to animals…her plan of a public meeting some Sunday evening in one of our churches, to be addressed by the President of the Massachusetts Society for the Prevention of Cruelty to Animals." On November 14, 1880, the meeting was held at the Park Congregational Church to hear Mr. Angell speak on cruelty to animals and the results of the society he represented. After his address, some two hundred people stayed and began the formal proceedings to establish the Connecticut Humane Society. From the beginning, it was agreed that the society should be a statewide group and not just Hartford, as "the needs of Hartford were not exceptional." In December, the group had a constitution with elected officers and a board of directors. On April 14, 1881, the state legislature approved the charter incorporating the Connecticut Humane Society. The first office was in Hartford, at the corner of Grove and Prospect Streets. In the beginning, it also was the only statewide organization offering services to children. When the state developed the Department of Children and Families in 1965, the humane society shifted its focus to only animals. Later, the society moved to Washington Street. In 1900, its first branch office opened in New Haven. In 1959, it moved to Russell Road in Newington. In 1998, a new thirty-thousand-square-foot, state-of-the-art headquarters opened, and in April 1999, the Fox Memorial Clinic opened. The clinic offers wellness care, spay/neuter services and vaccinations at reduced rates.

The society also has shelters in Waterford and Westport. The Westport shelter was established by a gift from the hero of western films, William S. Hart, in 1945. He gave it in memory of his sister, Mary Ellen Hart. The

The Connecticut Humane Society Headquarters in Newington, Connecticut.

Just walking the dogs. Doris Lipetz with Chucky Cheeks (left) and Jackie Rider with George (below) volunteer every week to take the dogs for a walk, to give them exercise and interaction with humans, during which time their kennel space can be cleaned. The Humane Society has hundreds of volunteers who quietly do a number of essential jobs for the animals. Both dogs were adopted within the week!

Westport shelter has been rebuilt over time to meet current standards and practices for the protection of the animals. In October 2004, the current building was reopened at ceremonies presided over by Hart's grandniece. In 2011, the new Waterford Animal Care and Adoption Center opened, replacing one that had served the community since the 1970s. To meet the needs of ever-changing times, in 2003 the society purchased a Mobile Adoption Center.

Today, the Connecticut Humane Society remains dedicated to the mission that "each companion animal finds a permanent, compassionate home." Thanks to the "spay and neuter" advocacy programs, the number of animals available for adoption is much less than it once was. The role for the society is now more of educating people on humane care for animals and how pets are part of a family. In 2011, the society had 5,507 adoptions: 1,687 dogs/puppies were adopted, 3,538 cats/kitten and 282 "others" (birds, rabbits, Guinea pigs, ferrets, et cetera). Over 1,000 came from out-of-state overcrowded shelters. By comparison, in the mid-1980s, the number was over 45,000 a year. Perhaps its most famed adoption was when Berloni, a trainer, adopted the dog Sandy, which he trained to star in the Goodspeed Opera's world premier of *Annie*. Berloni didn't have the seven-dollar fee the society charged, and he had to borrow it from friends. Sandy was indeed a star!

The society has appropriately revised its mission statement to meet the times and issues and to protect its constituency—the animals. The new statement is: "The Connecticut Humane Society is the leading resource in the state for companion animal welfare, enriching the lives of families and communities through adoption services, medical care, education, and the prevention of cruelty."

The society conducts a number of outreach and educational programs, including visits to schools, dog training classes and even providing a pet food pantry to provide quality nutrition to pets of people who are in financial need. Contributions help underwrite the society's programs and caring for the animals, as well as educational outreach. They should be sent to the Connecticut Humane Society, 701 Russell Road, Newington, CT 06111. More than three hundred individuals volunteer at the society doing a variety of jobs—walking and exercising dogs, cuddling cats, providing foster care and rehabilitation for animals. To volunteer, one simply needs to contact the Connecticut Humane Society at info@cthumane.org. All volunteers are interviewed and, if accepted into the program, receive training and are tested to be sure they know the "rules of the road." And that's how it should be, for the protection and care of the animals.

HARTFORD HISTORY CENTER

"If Hartford Is the Question, They Have the Answer"

The Hartford History Center (HHC) in the Hartford Public Library is the keeper and sharer of the history of Hartford, from its earliest days right up to yesterday. Where some institutions consider collecting items from a decade or century or more ago, the HHC knows that items of today have meaning today, tomorrow and for many years to come. Because it is singularly focused on Hartford, it is not distracted by other localities or issues. Carefully managed by Beverly Laughlin and, later, Janice Mathews, it is today under the direction of Brenda Miller, once curator and now the library's chief officer of cultural affairs and programming.

As with so many similar history centers, the strength of the Hartford History Center is its collections. Noah Webster, of dictionary fame, collected pamphlets and often annotated them. He donated his collection of pamphlets from 1743 to 1835 to the library. Elihu Geer established the printing company that published the *Hartford Directory* beginning in 1842. The Geer family gave its personal copies of the directories to the HHC so they would be preserved and available to share the names of Hartford's residents. In addition, the HHC has the earliest known directory, published by Norton in 1825, and Gardner's from 1838 to 1841. Any book by a Hartford author or about Hartford is probably in the collection, but more important are the collections of imprints, periodicals and yearbooks, as well as items that might not be collected and treasured anywhere else. The collections preserve, document and share the rich history of Hartford for over three hundred years. Here is the *Hartford*

Hartford schoolchildren become excited about Hartford's history in the Hartford History Center when they find they can look up where they live and see who lived there before.

Times morgue—the clippings and photographs of the Hartford newspaper from the 1950s until it closed in 1976. There is an extensive postcard collection, including Richard Mahoney's collection that shares images of the city through the decades. The archives and scrapbooks of Real Art Ways, Connecticut Opera, the Hartford Ballet and others are now part of the center's holdings, as are Gary Wait's collections of Gideon Welles and Lydia Sigourney. Robert Gregson of *Sidewalk* and *Thursdays Are a Work of Art* donated his scrapbooks, which record the art movement in Hartford in the 1970s and 1980s. There is an extensive poster collection, including Corita Kent's serigraph for Olmsted's 150th and a wall-sized poster for the Connecticut Opera's *Aida* at the Hartford Civic Center, complete with camels, elephants and "the cast of *Ben-Hur*." There are the extensive records of the Hartford Parks Commission, as well as thousands of glass-plate negatives that depict Hartford streetscapes at the turn of the century.

In 2006, Daniel Carey, town and city clerk of Hartford, under a grant from the state library, asked me to archive the clerk's five-story vault in city hall. Where Hartford might not have kept its records in acid-free folders, it did

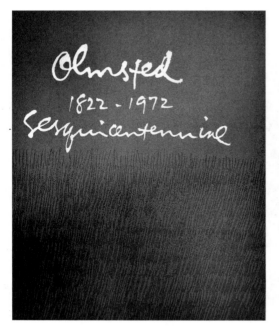

Corita Kent's serigraph poster for the 150th anniversary of Hartford-born famed landscape architect Frederick Law Olmsted's birthday. The holdings in the Hartford History Center cover from 1640 to the present day.

not throw anything—literally anything—out. As drawer after drawer was removed, to be sorted into record groups and placed in acid-free folders in archival boxes, it became clear that basically all of the history of the town and of the city was there. Mark Jones, state archivist at the state library, has said, "This is the most complete archives of any city or town in America." Highlights of the collection include the records of Hartford, from its incorporation as a separate entity in 1784 to the present; the record of each street being named, established and laid out, with notes on any and all changes; the taxable property records of all citizens from 1820 to 1943; Hartford town votes beginning in 1635; land records from 1639; and the trowel that set the first stone (1904) on the Bulkeley Bridge and that was used again to set the last stone (1907). Here are the grand lists; records regarding gunpowder, bathhouses, traffic ordinances, parks, streetlights—you name it. It was in the vault and is now in the archives. To date, over nine hundred archival boxes have been filled.

Once sorted into record groups, the question arose of what to do with the records, for they should be publically accessible—they belonged to the public. Conversations were initiated with several institutions about where the records might be deposited, the strongest interest coming from Brenda Miller of the Hartford History Center. The state library, which has statutory control of all public documents, was reluctant to have the archives go to a non-public or private institution over which it had no jurisdiction. In 2010, the state library agreed to the request of the Court of Common Council of the City of Hartford and of the Hartford Public Library that the town

TAXABLE LIST of *Samuel L Clemens* of HARTFORD, for 1874.

	ARTICLES.	OWNER'S VALUATION. DOLLARS.	ASSESSORS' VALUATION. DOLLARS.	BOARD OF RELIEF'S VALUATION. DOLLARS.
1	Dwelling Houses, *Farmington Avenue*		30,000	
	Acres of Land,			
	Stores,			
	Mills, Manufactories,			
1	Horses,	$150.—	150	
	Oxen,			
1	Cows,	100	50	
	Other Neat Cattle,			
	Sheep,			
	Swine and Poultry, over exemption,			
1	Coaches, Carriages, and Wagons,	250	250	
	Farming Utensils, Mechanics' Tools, over exemption,			
	Clocks, Watches, Time Pieces, Jewelry,	1,200	1200	
	Piano Fortes and other Musical Instruments, not exempt,	200	200	
	Household Furniture, exceeding $200,	1500	1500	
	Libraries, exceeding $50,	100	100	
	Quarries, Fisheries, Mines,			
	Bridge, Turnpike, Plank Road, and Ferry Stock,			
	Bank Stock,			
	Insurance Stock, *200 Shares Hartford Accident Ins. Co.*	10,000		
		Bonds 90,000		
	State, Canal, and all other Stock, except U. S. and Railroad in this State,			
	Railroad, City and other Corporation Bonds, with number, am't and kind,			
	Average amount of Goods for the year, with balance of good debts due me,	$10,000 *Chemung County N. of Bonds.*		
	Investment in Mechanical and Manufacturing operations,			
	Investment in Vessels, Steamboats, and Commerce,			
	Money at Interest, in this State and elsewhere,	30,000	30,000	
	Money on hand or on deposit, exceeding $50,	2,000	2000	
	All Taxable Property, not specifically mentioned,			
	Ten per cent additional for persons neglecting to make a list, and sworn to,			
1	POLL,			
1	Dogs, number and kind, *male, spotted, worthless.*			

PERSONALLY APPEARED, *S. L. Clemens* of HARTFORD, of the State of Connecticut, and made oath, before me, that the above list, according to his best knowledge, remembrance, or belief, is a true statement of all his property liable to taxation, and that he has not conveyed or temporarily disposed of any estate for the purpose of evading the laws relative to the Assessment and Collection of Taxes in this State.

Hartford, ~~October~~ Nov 2 1874. *Chas. E. Perkins* Assessor.

WM. BENTON, THOMAS BELKNAP, JOHN M. NEY, ASSESSORS.

In the Hartford History Center's collections are the town/city archives. In 1874, Samuel L. Clemens, aka Mark Twain, filled out his taxable property sheet, noting various values. Under "Dogs, number and kind," he added "1, male, spotted, worthless." (The dog's name was Hash.)

and city archives from the town and city clerk's vault be transferred to the Hartford Public Library's Hartford History Center, so they would be available to all. Jennifer Sharp of the HHC has created a finding aid to help one understand what is in the town/city archives.

The HHC is open to the public Tuesday through Saturday, from 1:00 to 5:00 p.m., and by appointment. The collections are non-circulating, and it is best to call (860-695-6347) or write in advance to request the availability of specific items. If Hartford is the question, the HHC is the place to start—and is probably the only place one needs to go. The HHC continues to add to the collection, for each and every item is a piece that contributes to recording and sharing the story that is Hartford. And if one has items, books or Hartford "stuff" or wants to make a financial donation, send it to the Hartford History Center, Hartford Public Library, 500 Main Street, Hartford, CT 06103.

WHERE IS THE *GENIUS OF CONNECTICUT?*

Richard M. Upjohn was selected as the architect of the new state capitol in Hartford on April 18, 1872. The working drawings were prepared, and the project was placed to bid. On October 10, 1872, James Goodwin Batterson was awarded the job with his low bid of $875,000. On October 17, 1872, ground was broken for the new capitol. On August 26, 1876, Randolph Rogers, an American sculptor, met with the board of statehouse commissioners to advise on the statuary to top the capitol dome. On September 7, Rogers signed the contract to create the *Genius of Connecticut*, the statue that would be placed atop the lantern of the dome, for $10,000. It was to represent a symbolic protector of the people of Connecticut.

Rogers was born in Waterloo, New York. His first large-scale sculpture, *Ruth Gleaning* (1853), was extremely popular, and over twenty marble replicas were produced in his studio. In 1855, he received his first major commission, the great bronze door for the East Front of the United States Capitol, which depicts the life of Christopher Columbus. The door measures seventeen feet high and ten feet wide.

The *Genius of Connecticut* was designed by Rogers as a classical symbol, with Grecian drapery and "Roman toes"—her second toe being longer than her big toes, a symbol of importance or of a position of prominence. She is crowned by a wreath of oak leaves, a reference to Connecticut's charter oak tree. In her hands are a wreath of mountain laurel, the state flower, and a wreath of immortallis, symbolizing long life for the state. Some say the wreaths are held aloft to bless the deliberations of the

The top of the lantern of the dome of the capitol was designed to have the statue of the *Genius of Connecticut*.

The recast *Genius of Connecticut* awaits funding to be restored to its proper place atop the dome. *Connecticut Office of Culture and Tourism; Robert Gregson.*

House and Senate. Rogers completed the statue in plaster in his studio in Rome in 1877. It was cast in bronze in Munich, Germany. The bronze statue was seventeen feet, ten inches and weighed 6,600 pounds. Both the plaster and the bronze *Genius* statues were shipped to Connecticut, and the bronze statue was placed on the dome in December 1878. The statue faced north, to the front of the building.

The capitol's general contractor, James Goodwin Batterson, on his deathbed in September 1901 allegedly stated that the statue was not securely fastened on the dome. Workers checked, and indeed many of the bolts that held it had rusted away. The statue was taken down, repairs were made and then it was returned to the dome. Following the 1938 Hurricane, the statue again was found to be unstable. The debate raged over what to do. The *Hartford Courant* had an editorial about its condition, stating, "It is only the question of a loose woman in the House, or a fallen woman in the street." On October 6, 1938, its head was severed, and the statue was brought down and placed in storage. In 1942, Governor Hurley ordered it donated to the World War II scrap drive.

The plaster statue from which the original was cast languished off a side hall in the capitol for years. In 1972, it was moved to the north lobby, where Glastonbury sculptor Casmir (Mike) Mickalczyk restored it. The statue was given a bronze finish and placed on a new pedestal.

At the 2005 legislative session, Michael Cardin of Tolland, under Special Act 05-1 of the Special Session, had $300,000 added to legislative management for a new *Genius* statue. A laser scan of the original plaster was completed in the summer of 2007. More funds were appropriated, molds were made and the new bronze *Genius* was delivered on December 17, 2009. An additional $150,000 to $200,000 is needed to raise it to the top of the dome. Where is the *Genius of Connecticut?* It is on the first floor of the capitol, awaiting a lift.

EDIBLE ORNAMENTS

During World War II, items such as Christmas tree ornaments, especially metal ones, were in short supply. Those that were available were quite expensive, especially for a young couple starting a family. This was the predicament Helen Hinsdale Faude found herself in. She was unwilling to have a tree without any festive decorations. Born in Meriden, Connecticut, in 1912, she was a graduate of the Oxford School and attended Yale University's Art School. She came up with the idea of fashioning ornaments that were actually cookies cut into shapes. They would be frosted with confectioner's sugar frosting to have a shiny white finish that could be "painted" with food coloring. When the ornament was finished, thin red string was used to tie it to the tree.

The first problem was to find a cookie recipe that would produce a cookie sturdy enough to be tied with red string to the holiday tree and also be edible and tasty. What's the point of making cookies if they can't be eaten? In a magazine, she found the perfect cookie recipe: one for gingersnaps, which could be rolled thin and then cut into the desired shapes. She then went to work designing the cookies: a rocking horse, a Santa Claus, reindeer, a soldier, a drum, camels and angels, sheep and elephants and more. The Santa cookie is six inches tall, the small ornament ball only three inches in diameter. After she was satisfied with the design, she used the inside of Land-O-Lakes butter boxes and cut them into the cookies' shapes, creating the patterns. After the dough had been rolled thin, a pattern was placed on it, and with a knife the cookie's shape was cut into the dough. The waxy inside of the butter box meant it didn't stick to the dough. Excess dough was pulled

The edible ornaments in 2012 came in fifteen shapes and were painted with twenty-five different designs.

away, to be used in another ornament. Where some ornaments, such as the reindeer, have the string tied around their necks, others, like the elephant, need to have a small hole for the string to go through. The hole is made before baking and checked right after baking to be sure it hasn't closed up.

Once the cookies are baked and frosted, the "painting" begins. The colors are the standard food colors—we use McCormick's boxed "Assorted food color & egg dye." With a clean brush, the decorations are painted on the frosted cookie. Some of the designs faithfully copy Helen Faude's original designs, while others come from the imagination of the artist.

Over the years, while the general production of the cookies continues as always, modern improvements have reduced the time needed. Her daughter Ann had a tinsmith make cookie cutters exactly tracing Helen Faude's patterns. A food processor greatly sped up the time and work to produce the frosting. In 2012, 125 individual cookies were baked, frosted and painted, representing fifteen shapes and twenty-five painted designs.

Who gets the cookies? A complete set stays in the house, and if someone comes and helps frost or bake, they also get a complete set. To the houses that have young children, a Santa cookie is given. If a cookie crumbles during production, it is consumed immediately. It is important that at some point during the holidays, the cookies are eaten. If it is learned that the recipient saved the cookies for another year, then he or she is removed from the distribution list. Here are the recipes for the cookies and for the frosting.

Ginger Snaps

2 cups flour
½ cup sugar
½ teaspoon baking soda
1 teaspoon salt
1 teaspoon ginger
½ teaspoon cinnamon
⅔ cup molasses
6 tablespoons Crisco shortening.

Sift flour; add sugar, salt and spices and sift again. Heat molasses to boiling, then remove from heat and add shortening. Allow shortening to "melt" and then add dry ingredients. Mix thoroughly. Chill. Roll out, so the dough is fairly thin, on an edgeless cookie sheet. This eliminates the need to transfer the cookie from a board to the sheet, which may result in the loss of part of the cookie. Cut the cookies into the desired shapes from patterns you have created or purchased. Remember to make a hole in them before baking if needed. Allow some space between the cookies, as they will expand a little during baking. Bake 350 degrees for about 8 minutes. Check the hole and then allow to rest briefly; then transfer to a tray to await frosting. The cookies must be completely cooled before frosting.

Confectioners Sugar Frosting

6 egg whites
2 shakes of crème of tartar
2½ 1-pound boxes of confectioners' sugar

In a food processor, add the egg whites. Mix egg whites until they form stiff peaks. Add crème of tartar and then the sugar. When fully mixed, take a clean paintbrush and frost a "test" cookie. At times, the frosting *will need a tiny bit of water to loosen it up. If one adds too much water, it will mean that later, when painting, the dye will bleed on the frosting and look awful. In about 20 minutes, the frosting should be solid and have a shiny glaze finish. If it does, proceed to frost the others. Some cookies are completely frosted while others, such as the reindeer, camels and elephants, only get frosting as an outline or for their blankets. It is important to try to get the frosting as smooth as possible. Let the frosted cookies rest overnight.*

Painting is a fairly exacting process, as one cannot go over the painted work. I use a small china plate and in the four corners deposit red, yellow, blue and green drops of the food coloring, with black (a mixture of red, blue and green) in the center. With a clean brush, I outline in black, for example, the rocking horse's eye, harness and hooves, and then proceed in red to paint its ribbon reins and saddle, which then gets trimmed in blue. The Santa is lightly sketched with the black coloring and then painted in.

Now you have everything you need to bake your edible ornaments, to begin a new holiday tradition, for all seasons or occasions, and one that will never be forgotten. And they are so yummy.

The round ornament of Santa riding over a village measures three inches in diameter. The Santa cookie is six inches tall.

ABOUT THE AUTHOR

Born in Connecticut, Wilson H. Faude, "Bill," was the first curator of the Mark Twain House, executive director of the Old State House for twenty years and currently the archivist for the City of Hartford and project historian for the Hartford History Center of the Hartford Public Library. For twelve years, he chaired the Connecticut Historical Commission and currently serves as a member of its successive body, the State Historic Preservation Council. He is a board member of the Connecticut Volunteer Services for the Blind and Handicapped, the Governor's Residency Conservancy and the Girl Scouts of Connecticut. For over twenty-five years, he has been a volunteer at the Greater Hartford unit of Talking Books of Connecticut and also volunteers at the Connecticut Humane Society. A graduate of Darrow School, he has a BA from Hobart College and an MA from Trinity College. He has written extensively about Hartford and Connecticut. He has been honored as the Civitan Man of the Year, was a CowParade artist and his needlework has twice been awarded first place at the Eastern States Exposition. He is listed in *Who's Who*. His *Hidden History of Connecticut* (The History Press) has enjoyed multiple printings. He lives in West Hartford with his wife, Janet. They are the parents of two children, Sarah and Paul.